Praise for *Letters from the Love Room*

Letters from the Love Room is an apt title for this wise and compassionate work. The author speaks of grief as it lands in her body, as it plays out in her life, as she feels it in the real world. Martin sits in the love room of grief and writes exquisitely from her heart. I love this book.

~Susan Lebel Young,
Author of *Food Fix:*
Ancient Nourishment for Modern Hungers,
yoga and mindfulness teacher

Letters from the Love Room is a poetic rendering of what we all go through eventually, if we have had the courage to give our hearts to another. There have been many books written on grief, but I doubt that you will find another of such depth and personal, almost mystical, sharing.

~Rev. Cathy M. Grigsby,
Interfaith Ministers of New England;
Chaplaincy Institute of Maine;
Religion and Values columnist,
Portland Press Herald

Letters from the Love Room

from the

mapping the landscape of loss

Corinne Martin

Made for Wonder
PUBLISHING

Made for Success Publishing
P.O. Box 1775
Issaquah, WA 98027

Letters from the Love Room

Designed by Dee Dee Heathman
Postcard Cover Concept by Corinne Martin

Photo Credits:
Nanette Vial - Front Cover Background image taken with permission of current homeowner Lisa LaNaux .
Susan Poag Photography-Author photo

Library of Congress Cataloging-in-Publication data

Corinne Martin
Letters from the Love Room / Corinne Martin
p. cm.
ISBN-13: 978-1-61339-907-1 (pbk.)
LCCN: 2017905984

To contact the publisher please email service@MadeforSuccess.net or call +1 425 657 0300.

Printed in the United States of America

Dedication

for you, of course:
Minerva Louise Martin
1908-2010

Table of Contents

Did you notice when I stumbled into the love room that first time? When I came home after you'd gone, and fell onto the couch? Stretched my tired feet toward the window's sunny warmth, and tried to rest?

I still felt you all around. You filled up the room.

Prologue

Here I am, trying to tell your story,
but it isn't mine to share.
I can't claim you, or even
the long rich tale of your life.
That was yours to keep, and now it's lost.
And maybe none of us really own
the journey we think is ours.
We belong to the long brave flowering
of the world unfolding one battered
stupendous petal at a time.
Perhaps we can only hope to bloom
in the small bright sun of a life,
to dance in whatever wind
blows our way, dizzy with
the wrenching joy of a little time
and an overwhelming love.

I can't go back to what is gone.
But your life still shimmers
inside me. The tangled trail
of our family still twines up
all around. The gauzy, lively room
we made out of love still lingers
long after the end.

Martin kids with Min (3rd from the left)

Min with Girl Guides (Bottom row, 2nd from the left)

Introduction

Introduction

My awareness of the "love room" began immediately following the death of a beloved, 102-year old aunt. Returning home after her funeral, I found myself still swamped with her presence even though she was gone.

I wondered about our ongoing connection and about close relationships: how each one is a kind of love room, made up of the truths and dreams and wrenching work that only two people can share. The love room seeps into our skin, settles into organs and bones, becomes a lens through which we see the world. But what happens when one person dies? Does the love room linger? Does it disappear? And what happens to the person left behind?

Throughout my childhood, my Aunt Min had been a bright star. In one of my earliest memories, I am three years old and crying because my mother has said something sharp, has laid a controlling hand on my shoulder, pinning me into place. When Min picks me up later, I sob into her neck. "I wish you were my mom," I cry. I can still feel the tears, and the warm comfort of her skin.

Of all my father's siblings, Min was my confidante. One of six children in a large extended family from a small Louisiana town, she followed an unusual path for a woman of her times. Earning a PhD, establishing a life away from home and traveling the world, she lived and taught in Germany for a decade before retiring. Both gregarious and solitary, she stayed single her whole life but maintained close ties to family and her Southern home ground.

Forty years my senior and living far away, she appeared in my life only on occasional visits. Over the decades, however, letters were the way we stayed in touch. Sometimes mine were returned with grammar and spelling corrected. But hers were exciting, bearing stamps and postmarks from Munich, Mexico, Jerusalem, Greece, and her home in Maryland. I prized and kept her letters. Later, I would find she kept mine, too. In fact, she kept almost every letter she ever received and many rough drafts of those she sent.

Our connection shored me up through the shaky journey of childhood. The gentility of Southern culture that left so much unsaid; stern religious injunctions; my parents' quiet dance with alcohol; an early abusive marriage and years as a single mom, had left me withdrawn and confused. I distanced myself from family for years, then began the journey of trying to heal. Throughout those hard times, the relationship with my aunt weathered the storms and stayed intact.

In my early forties, I followed my love for land and became a clinical herbalist. After a decade of study and practice, I moved to Maine and earned an advanced degree. There, Min visited our little farmhouse, helped work in the big garden and walked ocean beaches with me and my two grown daughters, Lara and Alison. After the deaths of my father and then my mother, I made more frequent visits to Maryland. My aunt, in her nineties by this time, remained healthy and engaged, insistent on being at home for her final years.

Once her last sibling died, though, Min became withdrawn, and I stepped in to help. Through many visits to Maryland, I listened and learned as she reminisced. Her childhood memories were bright and rich and I grew more curious about our Southern roots.

It was a sweet time for both of us. Her increasing vulnerability softened her sometimes sharp tongue, and she would often cry with joy to see me. I began to call her Little Honey, and Little Sweetheart, and she sometimes shortened my name to Co as we grew closer with the reversal of our roles.

Still, managing her care from a distance took a toll. As her needs increased, my own exhaustion and flagging health led to some hard conversations about the possibilities for my aunt's future. At the age of 100, she had a fall, and close friends gathered around so she would not be alone.

Min remained inquisitive and alert, celebrating her 102nd birthday in generally good health. Then, in May of 2010, she suffered a minor stroke and was hospitalized. She struggled to work at various therapies, but was unable to recover. While always grateful to see visiting family and friends, she eventually withdrew and refused to eat or engage in conversation. On September 4th of that year, sitting alone in a chair by the window, she slipped away.

But she didn't disappear. Her presence continued to be palpable and luminous. Our relationship was definitely still alive. Inspired by this, and curious about how the love room worked after a death, I began the tender journey of writing to my aunt. Brief letters just spilled onto the page. Over several years, loss turned out to be a winding journey with a timing of its own. And while I often questioned the circuitous process, I waited to see how the love room – that space we still seemed to share – would unfold over time.

In sharing some of these letters with friends, several noted that I have written as if to a lover or, sometimes, even to God. I have come to understand that, while the love room experience wasn't necessarily religious, at its heart was a rarefied intimacy that persisted even after death.

I began to think love really never ends. That the world is a soup of souls still engaged in some small way in our ongoing lives. That grief is a backward trek through the love room door. That we are never torn apart.

Min and brother Johnny playacting
(11 years old)

Min with friend (12 years old)

Year 1

The Love Room

9/15/10

Dear Little Honey,

After carrying you; after the frenzied details of keeping you afloat; after the end, and then sending you off; after tears and hugs from people who leaned into your light, now you're gone. But here I am, still waiting for you.

For, after all, could a life really just disappear? Could something so rich and tenacious just vanish – Poof! – without even leaving a small pile of flower petals on the floor of the world? Impossible. So I keep coming, in the dark and quiet unclaimed times, to sit with you, keep an ear turned your way. Our love room is still the place where I am so much of the time, no matter where else I might be. In the quietest of ways, you are here too, letting me lay my weary life down at your feet – your sweet, quirky self soothing me even after the end.

9/20/10

Dear Aunt Min,

I can't share you yet. Even though people are asking, I don't want to talk. Don't want to wrap up all my slippery feelings, package them into something tidy and give them away.

This coming-apart time is so wispy and thin, yet so much the realest thing: The quiet breath of the mystery of dying and living – the door between worlds, still open. I don't want to close it by trying to explain that the care and clashes and holiness of two people continue to thrive.

My love room with you is still hanging in the airy light, tangled in the web of my attention, still pushing and pulling with the tide of my heart.

10/13/10

Dear Little Honey,

Putting up clothes for the winter switchover, I grab a handful of scarves to hang and find one of yours: a bright, silky square of roses on scarlet and gold. Automatically, as if my body has a mind of its own, my hands grab it up and press it against my face. I am searching for your scent – the face cream you used, or your own particular sweetness, or the mustiness of clothes that hung in your closet for years. I am hungry for something of you. This time, it's your favorite color. Red – the fire, the unquenchable spirit, the warmth, the steely heat of your attention, the cutting edge, the joy. Someone said at your funeral that we should all have worn red in your honor.

I miss you. My body has known this all along, while I was trying to forget, trying to live across the hole you left.

10/23/10

Dear Little Honey,

I keep trying to find you. Working on the details of finishing up your life, posting your old photos on a website, planning a Louisiana trip to bury your ashes, going to Maryland to clear out your apartment. I am looking for you in the shuffle of papers, in the busy-work, in making connections with newfound cousins, Nanette and Lennie and Kathi.

But, underneath all this, my heart is a yawning awareness that you're not there. I can't imagine how it was for you through one hundred years of losing parents, brothers, a sister, friends, the way the world was before so many changes.

I miss you so much.

All I want these days is to slip into the love room – that little space we made together. We could sit and I could hold your small, delicate hand. You could squeeze my fingers and ask me how I am, or sing one of the songs you remember from so many years ago. You could tell me stories about teaching and I would listen. Again.

There are so many things I want to ask. I want to know why Uncle Johnny killed himself – if you knew how depressed he was. I want to know my dad as you did – when he chattered so much as a little one that you all called him "Peter Parrot" – before he was with my mom and there was no room for another voice.

This is the thing: I am still unfinished. I still need you, but you are done, I guess. But what does that make our love room now, if the walls aren't painted with need on both sides? If we aren't stitched together, using the glue of promises and faith and forgiveness to hold it all together? I am still in my love room with you. Sometimes I feel you there too. My memory of you still knows the best parts of me. Right now, I can't do without that.

10/30/10

Dear Aunt Min,

I don't know so many things: how to live without you, how to hold on, how to keep the small fire of our love room going when you can't be there, when you've already let go. Who will hold me up, I wonder?

Who will teach me how to age? How will I know who I am, if you're not here to remind me? You remembered me before I knew myself.

I wonder where our love room is now. Maybe it is passing – as you have – into some other realm. Or maybe it will always be suspended between two worlds – the one in which I am living as my body continues to be form and flesh – and the realm of holy shadows, of memory and ethers, of what has pressed an imprint into the soft, malleable creativity of the world, and then disappeared. For me, you are more than a memory. I miss your "here" self. I miss you.

I want you to know that this coming week I'll be going down to Louisiana to meet up with my sister, Celeste, and so many cousins from the Vial and Martin clans. We'll have a funeral Mass there, then take your ashes – what's left of your small body-self – to the cemetery, put you into the ground with the family you missed so much: Papa and Grandma, Johnny, Major, and Helen. This time, it will be your turn. You'll be going home to the soil out of which you were born and we'll be there for you. I believe you'll be happy – at least the earth-bound part of you that still might attend to such things. Happy to be home, happy to have your now-powdery bones settled into rest in a familiar place.

Together, we'll help close one long, rich chapter of our family. I can imagine standing there. I'll be glad to have brought you home – glad, and so sad.

I guess I'll wait to see how the love room works with only me left in it. But it's a lonely job you've left me to do.

11/12/10

I guess you know that I'm back in Maine after your Louisiana funeral.

Here, the larches are golden, spilling light into the pond, and the copper beech is bronzy in these, the last, bright days before winter settles in. I've lived long enough to know that the dark times will turn around to light eventually, but my body slips into the darkness dejected, wholeheartedly lost to what has been lively and easy and warm.

I'm telling stories about you lately, because people are asking. I guess it's what we all do when we try to bridge the gap, the torn place left by loss.

At the post-funeral gathering in Louisiana, we told tales that spanned decades. Small bunches of us crowded around a table, shuffled through your old photos, shared what we knew of the complicated lives, the comings and goings of our people. Now, I want to know so much more. You could tell me, if only you were here.

But here's what I have found again, that I loved so much in childhood and haven't had in decades: the jumbled, fun, confusing warmth of our big family, of people who love one another no matter what kind of twisty turns anyone has taken. Maybe there's something about growing up in a small town, living on land where your tribe has been forever, that makes things a little easier. You're never alone, which probably drives you crazy sometimes, but is also part of the tender web of belonging, of knowing someone is always there – someone who cares that you flourish, or at least that you're safe until you can get on your feet again. This is what you came back to for all your years.

I am eager to learn more about how far we stretch. In the meantime, I loved the messy tangle of being there, of belonging to that place and those people, even if none of them were you.

11/30/10

In the midst of all kinds of worries and work to keep your estate business moving along, there is this: I am still lying down on the floor of the love room, suspecting that you won't come back. But, like a faithful pet waiting for its lifelong master who has passed on, I am here on the slim chance that you'll return. My body remembers. My body can't give up. Maybe you'll reach down from the ethers of wherever you are and touch the hairs on the back of my neck, whisper something to me that I wouldn't hear if I weren't paying attention. I want you.

I want to lie in the old bedroom like we did when I visited: you in your narrow, sagging bed, me in the stiff, lumpy cot that smelled like unwashed hair and mildew, and that I could never tell you was downright uncomfortable. I want our breaths to mingle, our dreams and memories to rise up in small, damp clouds of family, fears, hopes, mysteries, love. I want to fold around me the threadbare blankets for which you and Helen carded the wool ninety years ago from Aunt Jo's sheep in the hot Louisiana sun. I want to feel the warm skin of the love room we were weaving together in that tangled work of trying to be real, heal wounds, learn, lean gently on each other, grow. I want the quiet and dark secrets of where you are.

How could you leave without me?

12/21/10

On this Solstice evening, this longest night, I am swamped with sadness. Your apartment has sold. I'll be closing the door, finally, to your long-time Maryland home.

But I'm afraid. If the place where you lived for forty-plus years, and where we spent so much time together, wrestling with love, is gone, where will our love room stand? What will happen to the wisps of you that still hang in the air as we tear things apart? Where will I go to be with you? As much as I groaned and complained about all the work of taking care of you, with it came something so special and worthwhile. I don't know if I can give that up.

I love you. I miss you. I want to send you a card and a box of little gifts to open on Christmas Day, but I can't. It's a small relief, this erasing of one chore from my list. But it doesn't balance out the greater loss.

12/27/10

For the last time, I'll be going down to your home. Part of me is excited to take this finishing-up step, pack what's coming back with me to Maine, give away everything else.

But I'm afraid for you. What will happen when those things to which you clung with love, habit, memory, are taken away? Where will your ethers dwell?

And I am afraid for me. What will I do without you? You are my final link to any parenting kind of love. Who will want to know how I'm doing, like you did? Who will remember me before I was conscripted into some guarded, acceptable shape?

Maybe you've left me clues in the litter of old photos. I see history in the making – my young face open, then shutting down.

More than answers, though, I want the love: the palpable thing we made, step by step, turn after turn, and are in some funny way, still making. The tenderness continues to throb. I don't know how this works, but I feel you with me and smile. Somehow, we are still forging something together. Do you think that's possible?

12/29/10

Oh, Little Honey, everything is coming apart. Are we tearing you up as we sort through what you saved and loved? Do you follow along the trail of all your things as they disappear?

Sitting across from the chair you called "old blue," where you used to rest and talk or sing to me, I am trying to recover from all the busyness of the day. Travel to get here, hitting the ground running, boxing things up, giving away little bits to your helper Esther, who keeps talking about you and crying, has left me weary and sad.

So many things are packed already: your clothes; the peach-colored comforter that covered your small body as you slept; and the family portraits all around the apartment. Your bed is stripped clean, bookshelves empty, mirror gone. The walls are bare. Only the big Jesus picture is left, and the piles of things to give away: lumpy bags of shoes and books; suitcases bulging with seventy-year-old sheet music; fancy outfits from your very social days.

Even though you'd miss all your things, I think you'd still feel at home here. Your presence and liveliness still hang in the air. Oh, how will I walk away tomorrow and never return? How could it be that I can never come back, that you will never come back? And what happens to me? I am still here. I'm still somewhere, but without you.

Well for now, I am sitting with you, scribbling in this notebook like you scribbled in ninety years' worth of tablets, and I am listening to the stillness. I am feeling you, loving you. Licking away tears as they slip down my cheek. Oh, how could you leave? Oh, where are you? Oh, how can I stand this? How can any of us stand it, the tearing away? And, of course, how can we not? This is what it means to be here and then to leave.

12/30/10

It pisses me off that you're not here. It pisses me off that now I have to go through life like the ultimate grown-up, with no older relative to keep an eye on me. I don't know if I can do this. I don't want to be "it." I don't want to be the end, where the time-buck stops. I don't want to be without you.

12/31/10

I don't know if you paid attention at your leaving time, but you did well. You did what you wanted: sat in your chair; stared out the window;

and disappeared. I wanted to tell you, just in case you couldn't see it from where you were. Probably you were too busy wrenching yourself away to notice. You would have been proud.

2/8/11

Dear Little Honey,

I've been ignoring you lately, turning away, walking fast by all the photos of you that I pass so many times a day. Not that I haven't been thinking about you, because I have – a lot. I miss our little visits together; miss our gauzy tent of time (and time-after). But I've been doing the details, trying to tie up all the "official" things that need to be done for your estate. As if any life could really be tied up.

Each thing I touch, each list of figures and accountings, feels like a tiny way to touch you, as if the faded notes you made for yourself are dusted with little flecks of your skin, the blood of your life still flowing through pages speckled with time.

Still, it's not enough – or rather, it is both too much and not enough at all. What I really want is more time to meander through the leftover scraps of your life, of our family's life. I want to open up the yellowed, curling envelopes and peer at your many photos. I want to try to put them, and you, in a time, a place. I want to know who those men were who are holding onto you. I want to know what you were doing in Mexico, or Cuba or Egypt.

I want to know all about your siblings: how you were with each other, who was light – I'm guessing that would be you – and who was heavy and dark, and why. I want to know about my dad and who he was, things I could never know because by the time I got him, he was used and shaped by so many things: the war; alcohol; what it meant to be a man in those years; and my mother's whims and ways.

I want to pick through the bag of old necklaces, the pearls you wore, and your mother before you, that mellowed from white into cream with all those years of pressing against your skin and hers. I want to pore through the boxes you left, open one at a time, and wonder about what you saved. But for now, that will have to wait.

2/18/11

Your 103rd birthday.

Oh, are you close by on this, the day you entered the world, so long ago? Are you drawn back to this sweet, green planet from which you sprouted? Do you lean down closer, to catch a whiff of familiar air, maybe to touch the gentlest finger to the flesh-of-your-flesh lives that still throb their small liveliness here? Are you pressing your sweet heart to the breast of the earth, to the heart of the life still unfolding in me and mine?

Are we still reaching across the mysteries of living, and of whatever the hereafter is, together? Maybe our hands are the love room, hands full of wanting and missing, disbelief and sorrow, all the good remembering and the beauty, and the going forth that I know must still be happening, for here I am, loving you, and there – wherever – you are, so recently gone. Your sparkle, the glimmer in your mischievous eyes, spills and shines and shimmers in the air all around me. Life without you – especially today, on your birthday – is hard.

3/22/11

I'm on my way South again, and I'm taking you with me this time. Somewhere in the hold of the plane is my suitcase, bulky with the photo album that is crammed chock-full of the long, wide river of our people.

Tomorrow I'll spread out all these relics and sit with Nanette and Jara, and we'll get to know each other better; we, these three directions the river of our family has flowed. We'll hunch over the photos, maybe laugh and exclaim as we find ourselves, our mothers and fathers, our grandparents, and on back. We'll trace our roots, understand a little more of our history. I'll be happy to get to know these living links to our rich and juicy past. Who knows how that will shape me from here on?

In the album, there are little bits of you scattered throughout the long family chain of beings. And there is also one whole glassine envelope stuffed helter-skelter with photos just of you. I don't know what to do with them all. You as an infant, a new, small face in the line of close siblings. Then a spunky, laughing ten-year-old tease. A serious-faced adolescent. You stocky, then thin and laughing, as one of your brothers snaps a shot of your new, svelte self. You seriously taking on the duties of teaching. You laughing out loud, your eyes on some good-looking man who is beaming at you. And you in China, in Greece, in Germany and France.

In all those in-between years – when you were traveling and mostly gone – there are no photos of you and me. Those come early and then late: you at 101 and 102, with me leaning over your chair, your head tucked under my chin, both of us smiling.

It has been six months now that you've been gone. Soon, I'll visit your grave. I'll lean against the warm gray stone, and imagine you in your little box underneath, all memory and gritty dust. I wonder if it will help any, being so near. Maybe it will feel like it used to when we sat sometimes, neither one of us with anything to say but loving each other in the quiet, sinking into the warm okayness of just being together.

3/23/11

In Louisiana, I sit with the photo albums. I thought I'd find you in the flat pages set afire by your smile, or that my newfound relatives would lead me back. It turns out, though, that no one knew you like I did. That's what the love room is, I guess: something only two can share.

Oh, who am I without you? An empty love room? Half of a throbbing heart? An unfinished story, now that my storyteller is gone?

3/26/11

Can I go back to what I never had, or to what I missed, even though it was there all along?

So many layers of scent, color, warmth. So-many memories, all slipping together and coming apart inside me: land, family, alcohol, hope, hurt, home. The many rivers of us, back as far as we can trace, and further.

Now, after so many years of growing up lonely, I have one hundred or five hundred cousins or more. Why did I never know these people? Why did my dad, who grew up so woven into this pulsing, tangled brood, not bring us here to meet them all? I have a small, sweet memory of funerals with many warm hands, hugs, stories of how we were related – all immediately forgotten. But, still, there was the warmth.

I thought of you, Little Sweetheart, so many times yesterday, as I listened to the names of relatives and the webs they wove, growing up together, neck and neck. All the Celestes and Jean Baptistes and Leons, on and on. What must it have been like to grow up in such a tangle of kin? I'm guessing there was a comfort that was bone-deep. Every face you saw had something of yours: a nose, a brow, a smile. It sounds wonderful to me, having grown up feeling so alone. But maybe it was hard to find breathing room where, for a moment, the oxygen was just for you. Is that why you had to leave? To find something of yourself that couldn't be claimed by someone else? That had only your name on it?

Well, you did it. You tore away. And still came back to touch down, to touch familiar hands and faces.

Now, in being so close to the knotted roots of our kin, walking the land where your bare feet slapped toward the next game, or prank, or solitary place, I am touching you, too. Listening to Jara and Nanette, seeing all the photos, I am both closer to you, and wondering, even more, who you were in the mix of so many. Maybe I'll find out – or maybe I'll find more of myself. For now, I am here with cousins in the small, dark room, listening to the train whistle blow across the fields, across the river. Maybe it blew when you were here, too.

3/29/11

Back in Maine after one more trip down to the lush land of our terrestrial roots and the tangled, prolific web of our family. I learn more this time, about Triches and Vials, Zweigs who became LaBranches who became Martins, all the living cousins and stories about the ones already gone. I even have some "double cousins," related on both the Martin and Vial sides!

Why did I grow up not knowing this wealth of family? I ask Celeste. She says that every time we visited as children, our dad started drinking, went off on a toot with the guys, and stayed gone too long. So my Mom refused to come. And that was that.

A liquid legacy then, the drink, along with humor and brilliance and piercing wit.

Yesterday, along with the free-flowing wine and pomegranate margaritas, there was the photo free-for-all. I wonder if you were there. We all stood around the table, pored over old snapshots, tried to remember the names of all the faces we found. They talked about your boyfriends – you always had a string of them. We remembered your flirtatious self: that sparkle in your eye, dimples flashing and the teasing glance. I guess all those men were drawn to your light, to the fire and the grace, the crackling wit, the surprising depth in an educated flirt.

I loved those things, too. And now, I miss them. I know you can't miss me. I can't imagine you needing anything where you are. Why do I keep talking to you, when I'm not sure if it matters? I guess I am getting used to being without you – a sad accomplishment.

Maybe the love room is like some of the old family homes, once so rich with liveliness and stories, but lately faded, falling apart. I'm still here, though. Maybe my heart has become the love room. But how do I carry this, the life we patched together out of love and effort, blood and history and half-finished dreams?

Well, my heart is large enough to keep stoking those fires, tending that holy room where we can meet, where I can lay down flowers and bring you strawberries and you can sing to me.

3/30/11

Dear Little Sweetheart,

It seems funny to call you anything. Any name seems just a fetter, pinning you down to what you used to be. But now you're less, and yet so much more, so absorbed in the Great Emptiness that names seem impossible, and somehow rude. You're far away. I know you still love me; I can feel you showering over me like the thinnest mist that nevertheless quenches some thirst of my skin, some need in my life. So I have to call you something, at least for a while.

4/6/11

Dear Aunt Min,

I've had my first dream of you. It was good – so familiar and natural – to see you. Just a little snippet of time, but it felt so easy and warm.

I was at a medical center, at a table outside where people were eating lunch and chatting. I tried to find a place to sit; others scooched around so I could fit in. A woman nearby said she knew you well. We talked about your amazing self and about your feistiness, too. We agreed that it wasn't enough to just mention the goodness, the easy part, because there was that other self – the flinty one – that sharpened you up.

Then you were there, wearing your long, voluminous nightgown. You took my arm. We walked along the bumpy, leaf-covered hillside and we talked. You needed to pee, so you lifted up your gown and squatted down. I said yes, it is easier sometimes just to pee on the ground, but you had to be careful not to wet your feet. We walked a little more, while you held me tight. And that was it – the end of the dream.

It was so good to see you, to hold on. Now, I figure that the table was our family, me trying to find my place there, a way to touch you through them. Is that what this is, the rush to know my new family? Am I just trying to find another way to reach back to you, to get what I've lost and miss: another way to come home?

I dream often about that land lately: the glowing green fields; and the rugged tangle of delicate things sprouting up all around the old houses. Is that what you were, in so many ways: a rugged tangle of delicate things, your fine hands reaching down into the dark and rich soil? You, the strong green shoot of a fertile family?

There is so much I want to know. Maybe now that you've visited me once, you'll come again. Maybe the love room will live on in dreams, in my breathy, hopeful sleep. I can wait for you there.

4/8/11

Dear Aunt Min,

In the cemetery, on my morning walk to see the pond, I pass the many headstones and think of you. And feel again a little guilt. How many days in that last, hard year did I wish you were gone? How many rough times did I slog through, wrestling with all the details of taking care of you, trying to leave your dignity intact, from so far away? How many crazy conversations did I have with your impassioned helper and end up wishing that you would hurry along toward your next life, toward whatever mystery was waiting for you, that final good-bye?

Now my heart feels weak and cowardly, but what was I to do? Trying to hold up the head of my own life, all the while keeping you above water; it just got to be too much.

I'm so sorry. I'm sorry I couldn't somehow figure out a way to do it all, for longer. I'm sorry I didn't insist earlier, in some ridiculously cheery and positive way, that you come up to Maine when you could still have made new friends. Maybe I could have been sneakier, tricked you into loving a new life here. But I didn't. I didn't, and you wouldn't, and so there we were. And now, here we are, finished. All the chances dried up, fading into themselves, impossible.

And yet, maybe it was just all that it could be. In these odd times, nothing is predictable, not even the planet, or life, or the money you tucked away, thinking it would save you somehow from uncertainty, from the kind of living and dying you didn't want. Nothing was certain, and then you were gone.

4/15/11

People remember your grace. They still need to talk about you. So much love welled up around your feisty, graceful self. Now, it has nowhere to go, so they call me instead. Esther, who is struggling to get the money she needs to become a citizen, and her mother, who calls from Ghana to talk about you. Rosemary, your elder-care manager, who helped to bridge the gaps when I found myself slipping as the work just got to be too hard. Peggy, who was there every day, and the aides who loved you and laughed with you. On and on, they talk and remember. You are hard to forget.

4/16/11

You're still one of the borders of my life: a sweet and sad edge I keep pressing against. Your black, flowered shawl – the one you wore in 1953 to the D.C. ball – still hangs across the back of the rocker where I sit every morning and night. Your photos smile at me from the desk in the dining room; the piles of your accounts are still lumped on my table – though somewhat smaller now – waiting for me to shuffle them into some kind of order. The emptiness of not having you out there, where I can touch or talk to you, is bewildering. But our little love room is cool with breezes today. And I am here in this small, stolen time, loving you, wishing for you.

4/28/11

I'm having my first spring without you. Everything is coming back: all the new, tender leaves; all the small yellow lilies in the woods; snapping turtles at the pond; the warblers. But not you. I'm holding in my mind, in my heart, the image of you sitting in "old blue" – the chair you wouldn't give up when Barbara redecorated the apartment and bought all new furnishings. I see you cracking a little joke, laughing at yourself, telling me that you're not sleeping, you're just going to "alligator": to go deep into that meditative waiting, as if you were a reptile on a sun-washed log.

You went there a lot, turning away from cheery chatter and the frequent problems, the ball-and-chain of details. Now, maybe that's where you are, on your own little alligator log, in the endless but not-too-hot sun, in the sinking quiet, finished with your life.

4/27/11

I wish I had been there when you were slipping away. I could have sat with you. I would have held a thin bubble of quiet all around us so the bustling busyness would have been shut out. I wouldn't have interfered when you were trying to leave. I would have just held your delicate fingers, let you grip hard if you needed to. Just waited, in the wonder of seeing you off, loving you so much. I think I would have been pretty good at that.

Would I have felt you tug away? Lift up, out of your body that had been strong for so long? If I had watched your face, would I have seen the change? The wonder take over? Would I have noticed any fear slip away, replaced by the sheer, exquisite beauty, the stunning holiness, the truest coming-to-ground, even as you left the ground behind?

Oh, I would have given anything to be there with you. But maybe it's selfish, this longing. Maybe you needed to be alone, to slip into the whispery world, beyond everything you knew, by yourself. And maybe you trusted me. Maybe you already knew that I could do this by myself –live here, in this, the tender tangle of things, loving the world, the work, the hidden diamond at the heart of all that's hard. Maybe what I needed most is this: you, trusting me enough to leave, to let go. So I can do that, too. In loving you, I can let you go.

5/18/11

I am on the bus, going away again, only this time it has nothing to do with you. For so long, every place I've gone has been about you, in one way or another: emergency trips; helping trips; checking-up-on-things trips; and then handling the details of finishing up your life. But not this time. I'm taking a little vacation, instead. Though maybe, in a way, this is about you too: about trying to recover from all the work, the loss and the pressure of living more than one life. I am so tired.

Would I do it again? Would I pick you up and carry you along, walk beside you for a while, then lift you up, fight your battles and pay your bills, keep an eye out for what you needed, even when you said, always, that things were fine? Well, of course.

It is a lonely journey though, this path you've left me to travel. A little lighter, now that I'm not holding you up, but the wind of absence whips too hard around me, when standing next to you used to be such warmth.

5/19/11

I still don't really believe you're gone. I've gotten used to the fact, I guess, but not the truth, not the reality. I race by your photos every day and your boxes are still piled up in the dining room. I've even thought, lately, that soon I may have time to look through a box or two. I've forgotten what's in most of them. It might be fun to see things again, to read a little at a time some of your many letters. Maybe I'll discover things, more little bits of your life.

I can't believe you're part of the past; you're still so alive in my heart.

One good thing: some Louisiana family members are coming up to visit me in Maine. I'll have a chance to get to know them better. I'm looking forward to that.

And I'm still working with the lawyer – you'd think he was a codger I'm sure. He loses things, then finds them, forgets details and talks forever. I just keep slogging along. Soon, he says, things will be finished up.

That's hard to imagine.

5/28/11

You're so much absorbed into the Mystery, so gone from my touchable world. I love thinking of how joyful you must be, sinking into the Great Unknown, the Great Heart at the center of the All. Still, there are leftover threads of you woven into my life, woven into the fabric of the universe. Everything lingers, I think, even if only in some discreet and unassuming way. There you probably are, your feisty and dignified joy, still shifting in the stuff of the world – my world, especially. So the new green of the summer trees, the tease of the mourning dove, the press of all the details of my life, are tinted with you.

I'm still thinking of Louisiana and of what comes next for me. I'm so tired of being tired. So ready, I think, to spend time being creative, or even lazy for a while, until my body remembers what it means to rest.

I wonder what your teaching years were like. Were they anything like mine? I know you worked until age seventy. I'm sure you were busy. I imagine that you loved the work and the chance to light small fires under students with potential. But didn't you get tired? Of course, life then wasn't like it is now, not so much frantic frenzy or endless distraction. Probably, there were different things that gnawed at your life. But you did tell Barbara once that you had never wanted for anything, had never worried for how you would get along. I'm glad for that, though it always created a little distance between us; you didn't know what it meant to go without, or to try to feed hungry kids alone.

Well, soon I'll have time to start going through your letters. I am guessing I'll find more of you in them, so many of the stories you hadn't meant to tell. I look forward to finding you, but it will take me a while; I can only do a small piece at a time.

Maybe the letters will help hold up the love room. Maybe the walls will be made for a while of tissue paper and onion skin, of white bond and note cards, of photos and torn notebook pages. I hope I can find you there.

5/29/11

I could say I'm getting used to you not being here, and I guess it's true, in some ways. But I am straightening up the bedroom now, plumping up sagging pillows on the rocking chair, tugging your black and flowered shawl back into shape, and there you are again. Or, rather, there is the emptiness of you being gone. Now all I have left is this: the bright cloth you wore, slung over a shoulder and the photo of you wearing it with your fancy evening dress. And the stories, of course – I have those. They are good, but not enough to stop the cold, empty wind blowing through my lonely heart.

Oh, the love room is a quiet place these days. There is me, waiting, and there are stories and things you left behind, and emptiness. Still, the love room must continue to exist; after all, we created it together, and I'm still here.

6/8/11

I'm thinking of putting away your beautiful shawl. I'm afraid the colors are fading and I want to keep it safe, keep it vibrant for as long as I can: the colors deep, the texture smooth and cool. But I also want to hold onto it, feel the silky fringe of its edges. I can touch this shawl, press its coolness, its flowing colors, to my cheek, wrap its slippery weight around my shoulders. I wish I could wrap your thin, strong arms around me too, but I can't. I remember them though, the holding-on-hard love, the joy of greeting and caring, the little desperate twinge of not wanting to let go.

We didn't want to let go. Maybe the love room these days is made of all the little ways I still don't want to give up what's left. I am still clinging to you.

6/12/11

Some of our Louisiana family came yesterday: Dede (Jerry's daughter, number nine of twelve children) and Pete and their kids, Emilie and Will. We sat around the table and got to know one another. Lara was here, too, wanted to meet the relatives she never knew she had. We talked about family history: who we came from and where we fit. They commented on your photos. Emilie recognized your picture, even though she hadn't seen you since she was seven or eight.

It was good, fun to sit and talk, to sift through the lively bits of memory and stories to find your name. I wanted to hear about my dad too, was hungry for details. How was he as a youngster? Why was he so susceptible to the drink, and why so inaccessible to me when he grew up in that lively, raucous tangle of kin? I thought their answers might be savory and strengthening bites of what used to be. I thought that they could shore me up.

It was good to talk with them – to keep you alive. The warm breath I used to share stories made all the flowers of memory bloom.

Oh, I want you. I want the self I could be with you. I miss lying in your little bedroom and talking across beds and years and dreams, holding hands across generations and so many different ways of seeing, our breath mingling in that small, dark place, everything held up by love.

6/14/11

There are so many questions I still want to ask. I want to know how things were for you in the aging years. How was it to be sixty?

And men; I want to know how it was that you had so many men. They flitted around you like bees to nectar. I could use some of that. Was it your sparkle, your charm, your flirtatious, flashy smile? Or your comfort with them after growing up in that tangle of brothers and the hundred cousins?

And what about sex? Well, I wouldn't ask you that, since you were so private, but I do wonder. I imagine you didn't give yourself away easily. Your morals were strong, your worth so sure inside you. But there must have been something. I have two photos of you with men at different times in your life. In one, you are lying on a sofa, your head cradled in some man's lap, his arm draped over you. You look so right-at-home.

How hard was it to give them up? Did they just let you slip away? I think not; you would have been hard to lose.

Oh, so many secrets and loves and hard times, now all folded up and gone. And me, still curious, missing the chance to ask you.

6/15/11

Today the jewelry arrived from the lawyer, now officially mine. I try to put on the Egyptian bracelet with its orangey-gold carvings and heavy amethyst stones, the hieroglyphs spelling out something I don't understand. But getting it on is hard – the clasp too intricate. Your wrists were so small. I put it back in the little bag and tuck it away. They are coming home, these things of your life, of our family, now in my hands.

I don't know why, but something about this brings me to my knees. I sink to the floor next to the bed, lean over and lay my head down. I am overcome. There is no emotion, just the overwhelming, palpable reality of loss, of coming to ground. The ground of the end, the ground of your absence, the ground of all the people who gave you life, passed now into who I have become, and into this – a small bag of precious things.

Maybe it is the realness that takes me down. After all the unreal things I have had to do to come to the end of this work – legal language to speak, hoops to jump through, the endless details – now there is this that makes it too much, or too little, or both.

On the floor lies the empty cardboard box from the lawyer, chewed a little on the corner by the dog. And in my lap, the bracelet that could fit me when I can stand to try it again. Waiting down south, there is the Louisiana homestead, and the warmth and green of our land, the remnants of all the stories still untold. Everything else, now gone.

I stuff some of Bodi's chewed-up toys in the empty box. He sniffs at it, drags it all around, tears it apart. For now, this is all the realness I can stand.

7/2/11

A dream: You are in a hospital, the nurses are talking about pureeing your food, and I have to decide if that is okay. I talk with them and say that you always loved eating, and that if all the food is pureed it will be gray and tasteless, and that will be really hard for you, so we should not do it. I see flashes and bits of your life, like movie scenes, and realize how much we'll be letting go if we stop feeding you. Then, I wake up sad.

8/1/11

So stunning and raw this has been, all the work of sorting out your things. Now that it's close to finished, I don't want to let go of you, but I do want to be done with the work. I feel you around me today, as all this is starting to wrap up. I imagine how much you still care.

And where is the love room now? I don't know. With all the frenzied last gasp of details on your estate, I haven't thought of it much. I've thought of you, of course, in all the pages of the daily details of your life that I sort through to get what everyone needs for the final accounting. But—really—can there be a "final accounting" of a life? What would that be, after all? Whatever it might look like, I'm pretty sure it wouldn't be numbers or lists.

This morning, when I woke up, thinking again about closing this body of work, this estate, you were there. You were wearing your old gown and robe, and you were leaning toward me. You looked both loving and concerned. Not worried, so much – for surely no one in the in-between world can worry – but you were paying attention. You were with me. You were reaching out.

Maybe our love room has stretched a bit, opened its thinning walls to the whole world: the world to which I'm still bound, and fond of, and the world of in-between times, where all those ethereal lives can shift and slide past each other, touching gently in the quietest of ways.

Today, I find out when I can write checks to people – hopefully soon. Then I'll be done – at least with this official part – and I can have my life back, lift up and off into the direction of my own going forward. I don't know yet what it has cost me to carry you; I imagine I will be finding out.

8/2/11

I am wrapping things up. Writing little notes to everyone, telling them the checks are in the mail, confirming addresses, writing a note about your gifts. I wake up thinking of all your little graces of thrift and shrewdness, love and concern. I have an image of you in your nineties, walking down to the little shopping center, keeping your eyes on the sidewalks, watching for change students dropped out of their pockets. You'd go back home with a fistful of coins. Now, we are the lucky inheritors of your frugality.

This morning, I feel you close, the small but very-present angel of care, watching over me.

8/5/11

Yesterday I actually relaxed: swam in the quiet pond, lay in the finally bright sun, stared at small ants tunneling under my beach towel, and grew hot. I felt my bones sink down, my muscles rest, my thoughts disappear. There was only the letting go, the water lapping, breeze freshening, clouds flickering over the sky.

It's been a long, long time since I could do that. And, oh, how much more I still need. But I can feel it coming. Something big and heavy, something weighing me down, pinning me into a not-very-comfortable place, is slipping away.

It might be you.

Funny, how such a tiny person, so light, could be so much to carry. But I guess that's the weight of a life: a collection of so many years, of longings and thoughts, joys and fears, and the motley, many ways to be. They don't lie easy on us. It's hard enough to live our own lives, harder still to do someone else's.

But you know what? I wouldn't have missed it for the world. Our rich, tangled-up time together was like a sweet, medicinal honey: nourishing, though not always tasty; giving life, yet costing something to digest.

8/9/11

I'm not sure what to do with myself. I've leaned forward into this time for so long – through your decline, through getting you help, into the struggles and the wrenching fray of your ending, and then settling things. Now, it's almost over; a few people to find for letters with checks, a few more relatives to get to know.

I'm having fun talking with Nanette lately; she is solid and welcoming and warm. And Dede is curious about herbs, going out now to harvest blueberry leaves for Pete's gout!

And I finally paid myself. After confusion and lost money and small squabbles, I transferred my share into my skinny bank account that probably thinks it swallowed a goose, or a small burro. It makes me a little nervous; how will I be if I'm not scrabbling around for money, if I'm not living with the sharp edge of desperation at my throat? Will I be mean, or worried about what I could lose? Will I take up, like a luxurious stole, the comfort of not having to think ten steps ahead, just to get by? Will Lara and Alison see me differently, as I did you – a little – when I saw that you had something stashed away?

Today I'm at the beach – an hour stolen from the relentless pursuit of lost letters, so everyone can get their checks. I am trying to rest. I don't yet know how to catch up with myself, or who I'll even be after such a long time of racing ahead.

But this in-between time is good, a necessary step in the unfolding of whatever the future will be.

8/14/11

Only three weeks until your one-year death day. Last year I was visiting you in the nursing home, trying to grab you back, anchor you to your unraveling life. Sometimes I came with Celeste and Lara. We tried to get you to talk, to eat, tried to pull you back from that distant place where you went all by yourself, when things were too hard: eyes that worked, but not together; walking that was too confusing; a bed that wasn't your low, sunken cot, shaped to your sleep-curved body; and diapers. The vulnerable chaos of infirmity.

Remember when we came? How we all stood around, talking, joking, urging you to suck in the pureed mess of whatever was served up that day – squished turkey, spinach, custard? Baby food. Except for ice cream. Even when you stopped talking, when you tucked so far inside yourself that you stopped answering most questions, if they asked whether you wanted ice cream, you said yes. If they asked what flavor, you said chocolate. You were saving your energy, I guess, for what mattered most.

Sometimes, toward the end, you would suddenly sing; all the sweet memories of being young and playful bubbled right up and out of you in a creaky-throated song. And you spoke French. In your last weeks, you answered questions in the language of your childhood, of your parents and grandparents, especially when they wanted to talk privately if the children were around. I guess you were going backward before you edged away. Your memories shimmered so much brighter than your now.

And then you were gone.

And here I am, still holding you, still grounding the shimmery, transparent space of your tender, remarkable life; of the things you couldn't have predicted but weathered anyway, with grace and not a few sharp words. Oh, your sharpness is gone, but the shine still lingers.

I sure miss you. Are you around, for this, your ending time? Do you show up for the anniversaries? Does the love room become a ritual, then? If so, I am standing here at the altar of what used to be, loving you.

8/17/11

I'm almost at the end of the estate work. I talked to one cousin on the phone who laughingly suggested that you might be chuckling over the hubbub of getting money to folks, but I thought you'd be saddened that they had to wait so long.

I did wonder about your letting go, though. Could you be worried that I'd somehow forget you if things were all cleared up, if all the duties were done, the money disbursed, the details scratched off the list? Do you wonder, maybe, if I'll scratch you off the list, too? Do you wonder if all the relatives, who were so linked to you by blood and land, talents and history and love, will just close the book of your life, tuck it into a small, dark space on the family shelf, and let it gather dust?

Was it hard for you to leave? Did you have some doubts, some reservations about letting go of the life you filled up so thoroughly? Was there a part of you still in love with the wrenching joyfulness of this unpredictable life? Did you have to wrestle with yourself to give up your plan for the last few years – to live to 105, 106, 120 like Moses? Or was it a relief to finally slip inward, close those shiny black eyes, and turn away from the world, sinking into whatever mystery came next? Are you settled now, all peaceful and relieved?

I have to say, I'm a little jealous. All I can do is imagine the mysteriousness that awaits, and there you are, already part of the nothingness that must be freedom.

Still, I do love this life. This morning Bodi and I walked in wide, deep fields that were thick with rain-heavy hay, black-eyed Susans, red clover and fleabane, all strung together with dew-silvered spider silk. It was like a dream.

8/20/11

Early this morning, I had tea with Lara's mother-in-law, Eleanor. I'm staying at her camp up the coast. We talked about dying. She might only have another ten years, she said. I thought about you and your ending years. As you got ready, did your memories empty out, leak all their juiciness, and fade? Or did some of them light up brighter? Did you love to sink into those precious times? Did you ever wish to pull me along, so I could taste what you had loved?

At the seashore now, fog rolls in. The beach is sodden, steaming under what's left of the sun. And there are dogs; one old Lab is furiously playing in the waves, crazed over a big rock just beneath the surface, a small boulder buried in the ocean floor. He is working that rock, digging and digging, jumping and splashing; pouncing, then resting;

circling, then coming back. Soon, I think, he will tire, but he has done this for the better part of an hour and is still intent.

I'm guessing that if dogs bring back memories in their getting-ready-to-leave years, this will be one of his: fighting the waves, mining the rocks, beating the water at its game of push and pull.

I'm wondering what your favorite memories were.

8/21/11

I'm so aware of endings now. When I talk with anyone, I say, somewhere in the conversation, "Well, who knows how much time I have left – maybe a decade or two, or longer, if my genetics hold true. But you never know; life is mysterious."

You're the reason I've started thinking this way. You taught me about dying, about getting ready, about being humbled into truth. About loving every small and simple thing. How to make a snug, warm nest out of what you used to love. And about joy; that, too.

But how did you prepare for your ending? Did it slip in sideways, that readiness, clinging to the papers you sorted and trashed, the things you gave away, the plans you set aside, the small talks you had with people you would lose? Or did it all just slip off your thin shoulders like warm rain? Did you not blink twice? Were you that ready, that willing to tug away?

I'm guessing it cost you something to let go. You might have even shed a tear, breathed a sigh. Maybe you kept making plans; after all, there could be tomorrow. You have to live until you die, right? I'll bet you did that. In fact, I'm sure of it.

8/26/11

Oh, it's almost your going-away time, your leave-taking day. I don't really want to write about this. All these truths, these mysteries, feel too tender and translucent to try to pin down. And how would I capture all these elusive feelings about your being gone?

Gone.

I am swamped with disbelief, sadness but also relief to be tying things up. And there's leftover anger with your first helper who drove us crazy, twisting things so no one knew what was true. Leaving you for hours alone, not buying you food – not even Raisin Bran so you could poop; how hard was that? And checks she wrote to herself, when you were still holding onto a bit of dignity by managing your own accounts. Esther said she found you hungry sometimes, so she shared her Ghanaian lunches from home with you.

So enough. We had had enough. I sent her off, but Esther stayed. She fed you, laughed with you, petted you, saw you out and couldn't be comforted when you left. You called her Diamond because she was the best.

8/29/11

It's been almost a year without you. I guess it's okay, in the way that any hard thing is okay that you have to get used to – aging, or cycling back to winter after warmer times, or the fallen fruit you lose to coyotes who get to the trees before you do on the first frosty day.

One year ago, you stopped opening your eyes or trying to eat. You didn't know we were planning to rescue you from the nursing home, bring you back home, duke it out with the doctor who wouldn't let you go.

Meanwhile, you were making your own decisions, taking care of yourself in the way you always had, without fanfare, but decisively. You were coming to terms with the end.

Inside your own love room with life, with the Great Mystery, you were counting down, having your final chat, making the leap. Maybe you became a prayer, inches at a time. But it wasn't easy, I'm sure, for someone so alive. Turning away from life must have been a wrenching thing.

It was wrenching for me, too. Those final days, so crazy. Those of us who knew you felt you slipping away. But the doctors and nurses kept saying you were not at the (official) "end of life." You could live for months like this, they said, or at least for weeks. So what were we to do?

8/31/11

I love you so much, but I have to lay you down.

9/3/11

Morning

Oh, could you have left, after a hundred years, without leaving even a trace? Surely there is some wrinkle in the world, some small pucker in the fabric of life, to show where you used to be.

Are you empty now? All the memories and longings and attachments, all the places where your own edges were married to the edges of the world, just erased? Poured out? Are you thin as a breath? A whisper? Are you there?

Are you still looking back, at least a little, to the place you took up? Your rooting spot? The ground of your presence? Do you miss it, or us? Or me? Is there a wisp of you still smiling a small, kind, curious glance our way? A tiny bit of you still between worlds? Maybe it is me that's between worlds – standing in this one but looking out into that next for a glimpse of you.

Oh, today the love room is a furious, whipping wind, blowing all around.

Evening

A soft pang under my skin, a weight in my arms, salt in my eyes, sighs one after another. A longing to just stare out the window into the empty gray sky. An impulse to scramble all my things into a bag and race off to the train, to roll past one town after another, going over the mental list of chores, my body eager for your joy and the fierceness of your hug that doesn't want to let go. Hunger for the love that always hangs in the air and settles warm around us, no matter what we're sorting out.

If the train goes fast enough, could I get there before you leave?

Well ...no. I may take the train down soon for a final goodbye with Esther, Rosemary and Peggy. We were like sisters; you, the mother we cared for together. Maybe I'll walk the streets, go down the little trail and into what passes for woods behind your place. Maybe there'll still be something to gather – flowers, or persimmons near the campus chapel, or the pansies you told me were Papa's favorite.

But you won't be there. I won't be buying you muffins anymore. Won't bring you little surprises, sit and watch you eat; hear you exclaim how delicious everything is, and wait and wait while you chew everything forty times. I miss those familiar things – our habits together.

But not the pain. Not that final frenzy of trying to get to you, then missing you by only half a day. And not the aftermath – the foggy disbelief, the emptiness, the lonely space you left behind. The sadness that you had to do it alone; the worry that you might have been afraid. I won't miss those things either. There are so many feelings, all roiling around in me now.

I wish you were here. I wish I could just call you up one more time, and your sweet, muffled voice could reassure me: "Everything is fine. I'm as good as I can be. Take care of yourself, my dear." That's what you'd say. So I will, but it's not so easy here without you.

9/4/11

The morning of your leaving day...

This time last year you were slipping away. All by yourself, you were churning around, tugging away from the womb of the world that had held you in place. You were going home – a reverse kind of birth.

Did you know that you were leaving? Were you intent, and just counting down?

Probably you were praying, talking with the Mystery that had held you up, slipping back and forth in the Great Communion toward your unbecoming, toward the restful emptiness.

I am so happy to be thinking about you, on this, your leaving day. My body wishes it could turn in your direction one more time. But, of course, that isn't true. If I could turn to you, again and again, I would. One time would not be enough.

I'm wishing so many things: that I could have asked you more questions; that I could have been more open, freer of all the twisty, needy times when I heard everything as a slight, when your sharp and piercing tongue met my shaky tenderness, and I withdrew.

I wonder what you would have wished. How was it from your end? Well, you can't tell me now. But we did it all – tangled and tussled, learned and leaned toward each other, laughed and talked and butted heads.

Now I am feeling weak, shadowy, only half here on this, the day the world broke open and took you back. Oh, I want to press my cheek against that small scar left by your passing and feel you close.

3 p.m.

At the frog pond, where I go sometimes to be alone, I lie on dry scrubbly ground, hidden behind small willow shrubs. Ants skitter around me, cicadas drone, crickets screech, red dragonflies dance at the edge of the pond, dotting the shallow water with their eggs. Sun and heat make a kind of womb in this in-between time of your passing.

No one really knows what time you left, but the death certificate says 4 p.m. That's when they found you, when the nurse who had just told me by phone that you were great – sitting up in your chair and watching out the window, having a good day – hung up and went to check on you; maybe to tell you I had called. That's when she knew. You were not great. You were gone.

It helps me to imagine that in those little bits of an hour before you left, you must have been peaceful – communing – stepping over gently, inch by inch, into the Mystery. You didn't struggle. You slid quietly, sighed and let go.

I want you to know that I'm holding the door open for you now, in this hour of your end. Maybe you'll reach through and touch me. Maybe you already are, and that's why I needed to be in a quiet place, why I feel so insubstantial.

Maybe it's a little like what I've read about Yom Kippur, when the gates between worlds – between whatever heaven is, and here – are open. Even though we're not Jewish, I'm holding them open for you now.

Today, our love room is all aflicker with dragonflies, aquiver with breezy leaves, warm with sun, sweet and sad with memories and longing and love, damp with tears. I am here with you.

Evening

After the beach and some work at home, I talked with my friend Margaret, and asked her to say a prayer to honor this, your dying day. She did, and it made me cry. I've needed to cry all day, I guess, but the prayer and the witnessing of your bright and complicated life, the holding on and the letting go, unleashed the tears.

Margaret told me about Yahrzeit, the Jewish one-year anniversary ritual of lighting a candle at sundown and letting it stay lit for 24 hours. So I'm lighting a candle now, small but bright and burning steadily. I'm setting it next to the picture of you at one hundred and another in what must have been your early teen years: legs bare, your rounded, girlish body perched in the open door of a Model T with a smile on your face.

The hallway light is on, too; will stay on all night and all day tomorrow. I can keep that going for you. I can light your way, in case you want to reach back, or keep the gate open if anything is left of you that needs to leave. Maybe tomorrow when I'm not so tired, I'll write down my story of your leaving day.

Now, crickets are ringing all around the house, the ripening moon is pale pumpkin through the hazy, dark skin of the night. The house is quiet. Everything is thrilling toward you, leaning toward your departure into the Generous Unknown that has wrapped itself around you. Everything is love.

Min school photo (teens years)

Min sunbathing

Year 2

Too Much and Not Enough At All

9/5/11

Oh, Little Honey,

I'm pretty sure you're too far away, and too much in need of the holy rest, to drop down here to touch me. I do feel you though, thin and wispy. Are you still between worlds, sinking and sinking into deeper levels of the mysterious Emptiness? Are you all glory yet? All light and airy shine? All melted into love? Or are there some small bits still unresolved, maybe something you are holding onto? Would one of those bits be me? If so, I want you to know that it's okay to let go. I want you to be free. I want you to sink into whatever light loveliness is waiting for you, whatever dark beauty.

Like the mystics say, maybe you have been absorbed into the great heart of the Holy One. May you sink into rest. May you un-become in the womb of the Great Surprising Tenderness. May you be free.

And the love room? It's still our share of the Great Surprising Tenderness, where sharp edges softened and our hearts braved discontent, our hands grabbed hold – sometimes clenched, sometimes gentle. But we never let go. We danced together, sipping the sweet wine of making the best of it all.

I don't want this to end, this time of remembering you, of keeping an ear turned your way. Even doing all the crappy details of tying up what's left of your life is better than nothing. I'm still afraid of the emptiness, the hole you've left. So this is what I have now: the stories – yours, left over, and mine, still giving birth. And our love room shrine, and the empty space you used to fill.

The world is a quiet, duller place without your crackling wit, your sparkling eyes, the joyful juiciness of your laugh.

9/7/11

I wish you had been able to go home, to be surrounded by your very familiar things. I wish I'd had a chance to love you more, or better. But you were tired.

What else is there to say? I'm so glad to have had you in my life.

I'll probably keep an ear turned your way, just in case you pop in at the most unlikely times. Maybe I'll sort out your letters, find more of you there, be swept up by the simplest, familiar thing and see you again. Your breath still hangs in the breath of the world. We are breathing together, even now.

9/11/11

One catch-up chore after another, I am laying you down. I'm not in a hurry, just doing the work. Trying to pick up all the pieces of my own life, set aside to keep up with yours. There are piles of papers to sort and file, school work to update, things to throw out or keep, photos to put in albums, plans to make for my own future. After twelve years of working for you, I am older, and having seen your end, I can see my own.

But I'm not there yet. I realize now that I've been carrying your aging and death as if they were mine, as if I were the one faltering and then gone, but that's not true.

And something new: I'm finding little bits of niggling anger with you for co-opting my life. You knew I wouldn't leave. You held on tight. Now I have to go back and see what I've given up and what I can reclaim. There are some things, probably, that are lost forever: possibilities, a certain liveliness I might have had at fifty that has passed me by. I wonder how things might have been if I weren't so used up. Still, the anger is all tangled with the bright, warm joy of loving you, and the grace of growing deeper into your heart, and mine. Of coming together to build the love room that sheltered what had been delicate and rare, and grew strong and sure and irreplaceable in the close-to-the-bone times. There is that, too.

Now, bit-by-bit, chore by chore, I am coming back to this body-home, without you. Maybe I'll find new parts of me, but I am sure even these will be flavored with you. Oh, I have loved you so much. What a grace this has been, the awkward trek through being, and not being, with you.

9/20/11

I don't want to finish, don't want to wrap up the sweet, tortuous work, the loose-limbed grief, the gasping emptiness. They are what I have of you; these, and the breathy conversations we still have in the love room that is coming apart.

How could it be that something so real – so bright and rich and full, so hard and fun and surprising as the togetherness we made – just stops? How could there be an end?

That spark and spirit and curiosity, and all the learning and changing and wanting to hold on, even all the niggling anger and resentment and the litany of complaints – how could they not hang in the air, rush just beneath the surface of my skin, be part of my bone and blood and thoughts, something I see everywhere I turn?

How could the love room not be waiting for me, that small, quiet corner where I can still look at my hand and see yours, reach out and feel the breathy air that might be you taking hold of me? How could it be gone? How could you?

I'm still not ready for the end.

9/24/11

How has the love room come to consume so much of my life? Why is it more real than everything else – better, even, than time with friends, or anything exciting that takes energy? Has it somehow gobbled me up, held me captive? Is it easier for me to live in the sweet cubicle of our togetherness than to re-enter the noisy, busy, throbbing of life? Can I leave the love room behind? Can it let me go? Can you?

Somehow, my life has become this: the bubble of our lives together, and the intangible, airy truth of missing you.

I sit in the rocker, making notes, end up straightening your shawl. I could give it to one of your friends; they did love you so much. Or maybe I should save it for someone in the family. Of course, after a certain point, family is just another name for all the people we love.

9/26/11

I think it would have meant something to say goodbye before you left. Maybe my words would have been less stilted, my heart less timid than usual. Maybe I'd have gathered up courage and looked you straight in your tissue-lidded eyes – your fading eyes – and said: "Goodbye. I love you. I won't forget. You'll live on in me. It was so, so good to know you."

I suspect that if I had been there, the terrible, thrilling mysteriousness of life-death-love would have flooded right through us – caught up all the tangles of our still-guarded hearts and swept them away: all the holdings, the awkward habits, any rough-edged memories. We would have been freed.

Maybe all this happened anyway, even though I wasn't there and you left with no one holding your hand. Maybe all the catching up and sweeping away, the emptying out, is happening even now. We're there until we're done – and are we ever done? I don't know that yet.

I do know something feels different lately, but even knowing that makes me afraid: afraid of losing you, of losing who I was with you. I am still kneeling on the cool floor of the love room, still swaying with whatever wind blows if it has even a whiff of your sweetness on its breath.

9/27/11

Maybe the love room isn't just for people. Maybe everything that lives – leans against another for long enough – makes an organic mesh of life, something just their own, that only the two can share. An enduring love room of habit and memory and continuing on.

10/1/11

These are the "after" times: after you're gone; after the first shock, the impossible wrongness, the certainty of you not being here; after the crazy, pressured work now that the details are all done.

I'm sure there will be another phase of letting go. Something new will bubble up that can knit together the brightness that used to be and the promising colors of a way forward. For even after a natural disaster, the first tendrils of resilient life poke up out of gray rubble to twine their green promise around what's left over.

Still, it's a pretty gray time now, an empty time, a blankness.

10/3/11

It's getting a little easier lately, the thought of you not being here, but what does that mean? Will I forget? Will you be just a pleasant moment in an ordinary life? Just a pale, thin wisp of the past? I'm afraid of the flat deadness of you really being gone. I don't think I'm ready for that.

10/5/11

I want to read your letters now, discover more of what you knew about our past, our family, the private things no one would have told a child or even a busy single mom. So many things I didn't think to ask. There was always, even toward the end, the little distance of age, of generation, and with you, the exquisite reservation of being such a private person.

I could sit with the letters, one box at a time. I have your own, that you recaptured from people who'd died. And those from your mother and father, Helen, Johnny and Major and, less so, from Fred and my dad, who were busy with families. I want to learn how they saw you. I've already glimpsed a bit of someone's distress that you were going off to China when your mother was having a hard time. You were the traveler – you, the one who went away.

What might I find, in all those boxes? You, myself, clues to the motley mysteries of our family, the rich and shifting pressures of time and change? Maybe I just want to touch you. I want something familiar, even if it is only your hand, penning any day's details: Helen called; Johnny's gout is worse; Mama is well; Corinne is struggling. What were you paying attention to then? What did I miss?

10/10/11

This morning the air is very warm, in the eighties. Bodi and I are grateful for a small breeze. As it touches my skin, I remember one of your final days, when we scooped you out of bed, pushed your fancy, commodious wheelchair outside, and sat you on the deck in the slight sun, in the gentle air. With your eyes still closed, you shifted your face to catch the breeze. "Oh, it feels so good," you said. All you wanted was something real, something your body remembered and turned toward so happily. What a gift, to be standing there, watching. To be moving you to catch that wind, to be loving you as you were loving what you remembered about life; one tiny, familiar grace, when so much else had been swept away.

Where do all those favorite memories go when someone leaves this earth? New ripe figs, straight from the tree. Dewy grass on young, bare feet. The familiar scent of a lover's skin. The way your body curls into just the right shape to fall asleep. The angle of your mother's arm as she hefts out breakfast leftovers to the waiting dog. The stink of the marsh on a fiercely hot day. Your brother's voice.

Oh, the love room is a teeming nest of small, beloved things left behind.

10/12/11

Some things you loved: strawberries; pansies; Shakespeare; good whisky -- but only a little; sunset; and certain men. Is the world chock-full of leftover loves? Do we all swim, every day, through the gauzy love rooms we've made just by living, just by daring to care?

10/14/11

Oh, my body so much wants familiar things, comforting things. To reach back and touch what was known and loved.

I wake up, dreaming of you. I am thinking of doing something big and wish we could talk. You were so able to walk that middle line, halfway between daring and stability. That's what I need right now.

I am wondering about buying the little farmhouse on Upper Ridge Road that I was renting when you visited us. That house welcomed me when I felt so out of place – or, so not-any-place-at-all. Good things happened there: you visiting; the kids leaving home, but coming back; holidays with friends; turning forty, then fifty and more; days walking in those woods, and across the very lush fields. And sitting in red clover and picking blossoms; watching foxes play in the spring; falling to sleep while deer settled into the long grasses that were beaten down by wind. All the herbs hanging to dry in those years of earthy work.

Remember how you went out into the garden with me one day, helped to dig up potatoes? You were so happy to scratch your thin hands through dark, loose soil and pull up whole bunches of Yukon Golds. You liked them so much that, for several years afterward, I boxed up some at Christmas time and sent them to you. You loved getting them.

And now there's a chance to go back. I wonder if you ever left someplace you loved and wanted so much to return. Maybe that was how it was for you to leave your childhood home in Hahnville and all those familiar people. But you found your own new ground. I don't know if you'd understand this, my longing to return.

As for returning to you, I can't do that. But here it is, a Friday afternoon, over a year after you've died, and I am writing to you. Are you there, somewhere, watching these words spill out of my hand as I think of you? Are you waiting for me to show up?

Well, here I am.

10/17/11

Another dream of you; you seem to be leaning close lately.

In this dream, I am working with a woman who can't eat properly. There are two other people helping me figure out what to do. We're so happy to be able to feed her – or you.

Year 2

It seems I'm still trying to save your life.

10/19/11

I never realized what it took for me to carry you.

Yesterday, I had a little feeling of not having too much to do. There are times lately when nothing is pressing. Of course, there are always piles of your papers to organize, and your photos to sort, but the piles are getting smaller. Sometimes I'm able to glimpse what I want to do with my own life that I couldn't see during all those years of taking care of yours. I'm looking forward to that: to taking up the strands of my own going-forward that I had just dragged behind me when I was living for two.

It's going to take a while for my body to recover, for me to remember that rest and play, and not being so responsible, are okay. It's a good thing, this little relief, a series of small recoveries, tinged with sadness. You did fill up so many holes.

Are you wondering if I'll stop loving you as I recover, or if the love room will come apart? Do you think there will be no place for us to meet, or that you'll be forgotten? Impossible. You will always be yourself in me, your inimitable self. I'll always be holding you up.

And anyway, how could all the things that make up even one life just disappear? All the steps taken, the innocence, the trials and sorrows, the joys. Surely they must make up the air we breathe, must be soaked up by the very trees and earth and stars of this world, even as they pass into the next. No matter what, you won't be left behind.

But, I have to say, I am happy to be coming to the ground of my own life again, eager to find out what's next for me. I know you'd want that. I imagine you showering me with hope, little kisses, and good wishes for great happiness. You are still loving me, of course. I'm pretty sure that part never ends.

10/21/11

Today's mail brought the final tax reports to close out the estate. I am still living in the bubble of finishing up your life, of holding up all the details until they're finally done. In the midst of the crazy frenzy of everyday life, this is still the most real thing: the quivery process of carrying you.

And the love room? Even after a year, everything else seems trivial, a distraction, an unsatisfying shallowness. What could be more real than the doing and undoing of love, the holding together and then laying down of a life? Now in these, the final, holy pages of closing the book of your life, I am still holding you up. My life has been given over to this: the ending, and the mysterious continuing on.

I guess this goes on all the time. People die every day, hundreds, thousands every second. Lives come apart. Love rooms are ruptured. Loss happens. Funny how easily we act as if it doesn't.

Here's the thing: You keep drifting by in little flakes of memory that settle all around me. Even when I forget, it all comes back. Today, it's the mail with the tax forms for all the people in your will, so they can finish their own bits of you and be done – or not.

I don't know what else there is to say. I am here. This is happening. I am still showing up. I love you, of course. It's the end, and somehow still not the end.

10/24/11

Now that you're gone and so much of your work is done, I'm aware of age creeping up on me. I'm thinking of retiring in the next few years, about what I want to do and where to go. Maybe South. I don't know why I feel so pulled to go back. I think what I really want is your life, or at least the life you had then, and there.

I want to be one of those children whose bare feet slap across the cool mud toward the next game. I want to sit under the old oak tree in the back yard where the rain lilies grow, lean against a brother and share all my woes. I want to pick blackberries in Tante Fafitte's field before the bull chases me through brambly bushes back toward home.

I want to gather at a funeral of someone we loved, hug everyone and listen to the stories about how it was when the older ones were young. Helen almost drowning in the old swimming hole. Daddy and the brothers frog hunting in a pirogue with a lantern at night, beaning a sizable alligator by mistake, dragging it into the boat, only to have it wake and start snapping vicious jaws. Then scrambling to get it back in the water, losing all the frogs in the frenzy. I want to sit on the gallery of Mamere Martin's house and card wool from Aunt Jo's sheep with you and Helen in the sticky spring heat. I want to sink back into what I didn't do.

Of course, I can't really have your life. And I like my own, anyway. Still, I want what you described. I think I can go back, somehow, if I move toward that place. I could be wrong, but I might need to find out for myself.

10/25/11

In deciding not to buy that house I mentioned to you – the one where you visited and I lived the sweetest portions of my adult life – I am thinking about what it is to lose what has been most familiar, most welcoming. Like I've lost you.

10/28/11

Your life came undone toward the end. You were laying things down. But sometimes you tried to hold on: to your car, that sat in the parking lot for a couple of years before you finally gave it away; to the familiar, decades-old coat you called "old tan," and wore even in the house; to the blue chair you wouldn't let anyone replace because it fit you perfectly. All those beloved things laid down the pattern of your days; familiar paths worn smooth by your tiring feet.

10/29/11

We are having our first snow: wet, sloppy, beautiful. I walk out into it after making pink applesauce – this year's crop of apples, so gorgeous and sweet. Today I got my grandson Peter a Halloween card. He loves music and funny, noisy things, so I bought him one that sings a little crazy song when you open it up. I think he'll like that.

And my hand was halfway stretched out to pick up the card I wanted for you when I remembered: Oh – you're not here. Oh, how could I forget? Oh, this is just too much.

How can I stand it that you're gone? What do I do with all the sweet attention I used to send your way? What about a Halloween card, or the call I'd make any other year, to wish you Happy Thanksgiving? How could it be that soon two Thanksgivings will have gone by without you, and more than a year since I've heard your voice?

I still can't believe it.

I think I'm asleep, in a kind of gray, groggy state, and someday soon I'll wake up to find that, Oh, you really aren't gone, and Oh, I can call you up and hear your ringing, happy voice, and love you fiercely again. Oh, I'm so tired of this.

I guess someone could ask, why all this grief over you? You're not a mother, or a sister. Not a lover, not even a close friend. You were, instead, the sparkly person who saw me. The star I traveled by when times were dark.

I still don't know how to live without you.

I am breathing into the love room now, trying to resuscitate something essential. You.

10/31/11

A dream of you. I am helping you gather your things so you can pack up and leave. The Nazis are coming, and we have to get you out. You're going through a box of bright, colorful trinkets and jewelry, picking out what you want to take. I am hurrying you along, keeping an eye out for intruders. Then I walk you to the place where you have to cross over and go on to the next part of the journey. A young man with dark hair is going to guide you. We help you around a stone fence and you head off with him.

Here I still am, trying to get you to someplace safe.

11/1/11

All Saints Day and tomorrow, All Souls. I know you're in there, somewhere between the saints and the souls. Maybe all of us are saints in some surprising and secret ways: what we get through, what we turn from, what shapes and sharpens our love for life, what we sacrifice. No one can really know what it takes for someone else to make it through hard times. Maybe you were an everyday saint. Maybe I am, too.

Lately, the sharp, searing edge of knowing you're not here is pressing against my heart, burning itself into my awareness in a way I was hoping to avoid. My eyes see a world that you're not in, no matter where I look. My ears remember, so happily, the sound of your voice. My arms know just how to press you into a hug and hang on tight. All these parts of me are afraid of the truth.

You're not coming back. You're not coming back? I don't know how I can ever stand this. Really, it has felt like you have just left the room of this life to go get something. And everything has been waiting, holding its breath, until you return. How could I go forward breathing the air of a world without you? What would that possibly nourish? Certainly not me.

I'm still trying to find you. I'm reading about the Bardo: the time described in Tibetan Buddhism when the soul leaves its body behind and waits and learns, finishes with its just-completed life; is purified, and travels toward its next incarnation. But the Bardo only gives you forty-nine days, and that's not enough. Here it is, more than a year since you've been gone, and I still feel you. I don't know if you're really here, but I can't imagine two lives could be so intertwined and rooted in the heart and then just come apart. So I'll keep reading. Maybe the mystics have more to say, or maybe there's nothing to say. Maybe there's only this: the odd, remarkable, unbelievable, stunning reality of being here, and then gone. What?

Our love room is thick with questions, and the still-shocking possibility of the end.

11/2/11

I am still wanting what I think you had, what I see in all the old family photos. Lately, I am watching TV a lot, old reruns of "The Waltons." I want to be there. I want to be surrounded by all those bodies, with those squabbling, jostling, laughing, teasing, argumentative family folk pressing against each other. You must have had that. With so many siblings, and so many more cousins, no one could be too high, or too lost, or too hidden, at least not for long. That's what I want.

I want the truth of being called on my twisty ways, on my uppity self and my down-putting self. I want the grace of being just what I am – the grace that is easier, I think, if so many people know you well, expect you to show up. You are lifted up, but not too high.

I think you had that. You probably left hoping to get away from it a little, but you always went back. And I don't think they let you get away with much.

I hope this is true – that you had those things.

And since I can't sink into the television and become just another Walton, or go back into that life out of which you rose up, it seems now like I'm on my own. I will have to count on something else to keep me straight. I don't know what that will be.

11/5/11

I'm missing our people. I'm missing our land: the low, damp, flat, ridiculously fertile soil; the green, brushy growth; heady, sweet-scented flowers; the gnarly tangle of family, all enmeshed.

I wonder if any of them remembered yesterday that it was your burial time. One year exactly since we gathered together to see your body off, to celebrate your particular life, and the rich, quirky, graced lives of all our people. Your name, your face, might have popped into someone's head, or heart.

It's so good to turn to you now, to the breathy, airy space where you used to be. I'm so sorry you're not here. I'm so glad you were, for such a long time.

I imagine our loved ones, those already passed on, all hanging together like little wispy clouds, right over your small box of ashes. Maybe you're with them now.

11/6/11

Antidepressants. Huh. I don't know what you'd think of this, me taking medication to ease the raw emptiness of losing you. You were so strong, so used to letting go of those you loved. One hundred-plus years is a long time to practice emptiness. But I'm not so good at it yet.

I do remember seeing you at the funeral home after Grandma died. I was sixteen, feeling lost as usual, slipping by the casket to look at her long, stiff, not-very-natural face, pressing a finger to her skin that seemed so real but turned out to be cold. You flashed in, just off the plane from Germany, flung yourself into someone's arms, screamed "Mama!" They slipped you off into some room I couldn't enter. Later, you came back, but I don't remember much more, except that your presence there did something to the room. Things changed after that.

And something happened to me, too. I don't know why, but that slipping away of the woman who felt like my personal angel, and your own wrenching cry, brought out something in me that persists to this day: my public self that could rise up to whatever needed to be done instead of staying tucked into a corner or meandering down a dirt road alone.

You were there, at that birth of my alternate self, my competent self. I don't know if you noticed, but it was that self, I think, that was able to do the so-many details of taking care of you in your last years. I wonder now what that might have cost me, that new and able self. What would it have been like to say "no," to fall into a heap, or someone's arms? To come undone? Maybe that's what I'm doing now: falling into the arms of need; pressing away from the rawness of loss;, taking a little solace in a pill. Well...we'll see how that goes.

And you? I'm still talking to you, not about you. One little pronoun makes such a difference. If I'm talking to you, you must be there. With just this little word, I'm calling you up.

I wonder who will see me out when I am ready to leave. It won't be you. Or maybe it will. As you got closer to your ending time, you called out for your own mother. I am guessing she was there waiting for you. Will I call for my own mother too on my last day? Or will I call for you? I'm hoping not to find out anytime soon. But I'm betting you'll be there as I'm laying it all down, this juicy life and whatever breathy shards of the love room follow me to that last day.

11/9/11

Sitting in the rocking chair, I get up to adjust your shawl that is hanging behind me. Maybe I should just pack it away. I don't think about it much anymore, but I have gotten used to it being there. I am not ready to let it go, to not see it. I'm not ready to let go of you, either.

11/10/11

How am I supposed to live through this – the ragged, raw, pressing-down of grief, of really getting it that you're gone? That everything can be gone? Aside from just pretending it's not true, aside from turning away and keeping myself entertained – which isn't really working anyway – what do I do? The world seems a harsh and demanding place these days; nowhere I want to be. The love room walls, tattered in a hard, mean wind.

11/11/11

Loss. Salt on the tenderest of wounds.

11/12/11

Bodi and I walked home from the woods, stopped at the little garden plot where everything was frosted and beaten down. I pulled up tomato cages under the pale sun, untangled stiff, dead stalks that had woven themselves through the wires. It felt so good to do one small, earthy thing, alone and quiet, my body leaning toward the sun as if it was nectar and I were parched.

And you, and what's left of us? You are the sliver of sweetness at the edge of so much that's hard: the ending of things, including you; the coming cold; the loss of light; the garden that has bloomed up already and now slumps downward, tired and spent; my own fatigue.

If you were here, I could talk with you. Instead, I'm sitting now in the bedroom window where sun paints my arms, writing to you even though I have nothing much to say.

11/13/11

Tonight I watched a movie about a man whose son had died while hiking. The father took a months-long walk to lay ashes at different places along the road his son had traveled. What an amazing thing it could be to take that time to just walk, to just do what you want to do when you're grieving, which is nothing, which is being alone. Not trying to pretend. Not getting caught up in all the stupid, meaningless details that gulp down your life, press down the truest thing that is happening: the empty, tearing, coming-undone-ness of loss.

I think you'd understand. I saw you sit for hours in a chair after your sister died. You sat and stared into space, stopped paying bills or dressing or getting together with friends. You two were the last of the siblings – and then she was gone, and you were the last of the last: a quiet, lonely fact.

I told a friend recently that the grief, this awful, yawning hole, is a transparent bubble surrounding my whole life. Everything I do is done within that invisible enclosure. And it is terrible, but is also the only thing I want, the best thing I do lately. I want to sit here with you, with your absence. I want to not talk, not respond to any needs. I want to stare off into space, wait until all the noises quiet down, all the people are gone, and see, and feel, what's left. It might be you. Or the palpable shudder of the world without you. That might be all I can bear.

Is this depression? Maybe. But it's also the only sensible thing to do when the world tears open and takes someone back.

Maybe, someday soon, I'll want to move again. Maybe the sun will inspire me and I'll finally rise up and walk lightly and laugh. But not right now.

11/15/11

In the dark, I wake up thinking about you, and the love room, and the Great Letting Go I am going through these days. It seems that losing you has triggered the breaking open of all those love rooms I've ever had, and then lost, in life. I don't know if I can stand it all.

11/16/11

Tonight the telephone rings late and, for just a moment, my body tenses. I am sure it's about you: some emergency, some long-winded, scary report from your helper, one more awful complication. Of course, it isn't, but I wish it were. Then, you'd still be there. And that would be good.

I guess love never stops waiting and the love room is never wholly gone.

11/18/11

All I want to do is write to you. The ink that flows out of this pen, out of my hand and heart, is a thin, curving line that tethers me to you.

Lately, the only people I want to be around are those who know what grieving is, who can understand that I'm living inside a bubble. A bubble of what? Shock? Reality? Loss? Love, welling up and flooding over? Anger? Depression? Hunger for time alone? Need for comfort? Exhaustion? Intolerance of anything shallow, or too cheery? Yes.

How could it be that we think love is tidy, that emotions are served up one simple feeling at a time? How could I be so full of pain and still walk around pretending to be easy? How can I stand up at all?

This morning the sun is up, low in the sky, but not so warm. A cold wind blows, twitching bare tree limbs into circles, making crazy shadows of scrambled light.

I need more than this. I need real warmth, steady and bright. I need something gentle and sure. I need to rest, lean against what's dependable, close my eyes and drop the fear that when I open them again, you won't be there. You'll be gone. Everything will be gone. I need a quiet and good place.

For now, the love room will have to do.

11/19/11

What does it say about me, that I'm still feeling most at home with you when you're not even here anymore? Does it mean that I don't have a life? That I was so taken with you and your care that there was no room for anyone else, as my daughters complained in your last years? And what man might have been there for me, but passed by unnoticed while I was wrestling with you? Was laying down my heart, over and over, to see you through to the end? Now, here I am with a decade-worth of tiredness, and the hole you left, and the pale, fluttery questions of what might have happened if I'd been free.

Can I be sad and mad that I gave you all those years? Well, no. Can I wonder about myself, about what comes next; how I will finally, if ever, lay you down, and what will happen then? Absolutely.

11/21/11

Another holiday is rolling around, another time I think of you. I'm going down to Louisiana again to see our people. I am trying, still, to get to know some of them; I am trying to figure out who they are and where I might fit in that tight clutch of folk. In these, my more-than-middle-aged years, I am thinking ahead, trying to see how and where my life can lay itself out, what would shore me up. Stretch me in good and helpful ways. What would keep sparking my curiosity and give me a place to rest, a spot where I can stand and keep loving the world.

I want to know if all those old, green, fecund dreams, those pristine memories and longings, make any kind of sense, can land me anywhere real, or be laid down into a road that will take me home.

11/22/11

I'm going to the bayous. Nanette has asked if I'd like to take a boat ride with her back to the water. Little does she know that's what my little-girl heart always yearned for – where I've been longing to go in all my trips to Louisiana, so I could soak up those places that were so much a part of your life and my dad's. I have pictures of you and your girlhood friends, poling yourselves along the edges of the bayou on a raft, still wearing your school uniforms, stockings rolled down, ties askew, hair wild. You, looking serious; your cousin, Zo, laughing out loud; all of you so at home on the water.

Maybe, somehow, those dark, slow-moving waterways will stir up something, take me back to what could have been.

Maybe I'll spot you there, or see my dad and all your brothers hunting for frogs at night. I'll let you know what I find.

11/25/11

We fly over Washington and all I can think about is visiting you: those familiar places I walked by so often when I needed a break from the long hours of sitting in that cramped apartment, watching you sleep, or making up questions to ask so we'd have something to say. What was I to do with the edginess of caring, of being tired and wanting to fix things, and not knowing how? Me, wanting so much for you, and you, just wanting to be quiet and ponder the last of your life. Neither one of us knowing exactly what to do with each other, but wanting to stick it out, be true to that force that had bound us together for so long.

11/26/11

Here I am again in Hahnville, trying to sink into what I could have had, trying to wriggle my way in through the crack you left in this world. You are my open door. There are still people here who are linked to you by blood and stories, so I'm using you, I guess, to get back in. The small, steady light you shed is my beacon, forward and backward along the path. We'll see how that works.

Earlier today, there was an annual cookie-baking fest with all the cousins; the same recipe, used for dozens of years, the results boxed up to give to needy folks for the holidays. Me, still trying to juggle names and degrees of cousin-hood – and having fun.

Now, the train whistle hoots somewhere close by, that pulse of childhood nights I spent in Grandma's house with the dark so absolute I kept touching my eyes to make sure they were really open. I loved that sound of something far off, and possible.

You were that for me: sounding out what could be possible. Now, the train, the sweet, heavy scent of dark soil, of water somewhere close by, flowers nodding in trees still lush, even on this November night, the gentle air – all rise up and wrap around me. The love room tonight is chock-full of so many beloved things.

11/27/11

A night jumbled with dreams of all the cousins pressed under my skin. Nanette and Dede and Will, and the clot of noisy kin, so close I can't untangle them even from my first-thing-in-the-morning prayers that start out empty and end up halfway through in some cousin's remembered question from yesterday.

These – my people – are seeping into me like the land has soaked into the outer layers of my awareness until it is hard to tell where they – the kin, or the land – stop, and the light, quivering flicker of what I am, all by myself, begins. How do I sort these out?

Still, I love the warmth, the open doors and arms I can just walk into. You loved that, too; you always returned to them. But you also held on hard to your need to be solitary, to be just with yourself. Maybe there's a way to squiggle down into this crowd and be one of the gang, and to stand on my own too. I guess that's what we all need, really, to live in any kind of closeness.

Today, I'll be walking as many country roads as I can. And visiting you in the cemetery, where your soft, gritty ashes lie. Maybe I'll feel you there.

11/28/11

Morning

I want to visit you again. Yesterday's flash trip to the graveyard, in the cold, stiff wind, under that scowling gray sky, with Celeste at my side, just wasn't enough. I know she loved you, but she doesn't indulge in sentiment much, wasn't heart-to-heart with you in the way I was, in all those years toward the end of your life.

The cemetery is surreal – all the flat, whitewashed graves, surrounded by the giant, snaking arms of the chemical plants that have bought up all the land they could get. Nothing really restful about your resting place.

We found your name, tucked the red poinsettia we brought near your headstone. It shook in the strong wind, a small bright flag. You felt so close. Just not near enough to touch.

Celeste noted that your death date hasn't yet been engraved. I'll have to check on that.

Now the sun is out, and we're off to New Orleans to have lunch with Dede and Nanette. I think you'd enjoy seeing them, the warm and lively cousins. Maybe you'll join us there.

Evening

At lunch, Nanette talked about the rich tangle of seven generations of Vial/Martin families living in the same place. She used a napkin to draw a tree of the family ties, the thicket of loves from which you had to pull away so you could make your own way. That must have been hard, for the love room, it turns out, is a gigantic place, holding up all those people for so long: astounding, rich, enmeshed.

11/29/11

On the way home to Portland, the plane stops at the Baltimore airport. A gray rain snakes down the window glass, fog obscuring anything beyond the silvery body of the plane. You could be out there, just behind the smoky bank of mist.

Oh, are you huddled into your warm, blue chair, waiting for me? Did I forget to tell you I was passing by? Is there some shard left of you in your little former home?

If I were with you, it would be a quiet day. I might curl up on the narrow cot in your room and read right through the new novel I bought, or sit in the chair across from you and watch you nap. That would be so good.

Instead, we lift off again, though I haven't done what I came for, what my body usually does. I am supposed to be moving toward you, not farther away. How can I leave without you? None of this makes sense.

The plane lurches, side to side. It could just drop out of the soggy gray sky. I could sink down to you. But what would the love room be then? Shattered.

No, I'm not ready to quit, even if it means being without you. I want the sunshine of my own life; the rest of whatever there is for me. I know you'd want that, too. So up we go, leaving the rough, dark ride behind, into blue sky, into light.

And now that we're gone, I'm okay. I can't go back. But being so near was just too hard, too much. So close to possible.

11/30/11

The sweet gauzy bubble of being with you seems to come in little waves these days, tugged into place by something we shared. This morning, back home in Maine, I walked by the post office where I went so many times to send things out to you – little packages at holiday times, cards, and the latest pictures of Peter. And those many trips to settle all the estate stuff, tracking down lost checks and tax papers to close everything out. Today, there you are.

12/1/11

Tonight I lean over to light the tiny candle on my bedroom altar that's a jumble of so many things I love: seashells; a picture of a polar bear; a tiny, framed angel icon in a little frame; the photo of me at one-year old, held up by my dad. The carving of the Profound Buddha absorbing the sorrows of the world; the collage Lara made for Mother's Day; an osprey feather. And a photo of you with your impish smile, in that bright red sweater, on your one-hundredth birthday.

Looking at your picture, I glance away. I don't want to look at you now. I can't believe you're really gone. I don't want to.

If I were Buddhist, I'd probably just stare and stare – a meditation on letting go, on nothingness. But even though I think there might be merit in that, I turn away. I don't want to know. The realness is too jarring, too much. I choose the blurry unknowing, my fogged-over memory, instead. The love room poured out is too much to think about. Too much to know.

12/2/11

Grief: the poignant, beautiful sadness swimming underneath every other thing. I want to turn back. I want to wait for you. I want to hold my breath, just in case your tiniest whisper could press against my skin, wrap around me like a cool mist, and I could lap it up.

12/3/11

This time last year, I was visiting you – or rather, not you, but the chock-full shell of the life you had left behind. Every other week was a flash trip down to Maryland, hitting the ground running, opening the door to your condo, dumping my suitcase, whipping off coat and scarf and gloves and diving in.

It makes me tired just to think of it, and sad. But the best thing? I was knee-deep in you. Touching so many familiar things, I could pretend you were just away. I could drown in the work and forget why I was doing it.

Now, I want to sink into the memory of that time and stretch it out, unfold that cramped, busy press to get things done. I wish I had worked more slowly. I wish I could have spread out that impossible jumble of chores and done them one at a time. Gone through the tangle of jewelry, wondering about each piece. Fingered the fantastic costumes you wore when you were dazzling -- and imagine you in them.

And reading the letters – I did save most of them. Someday I'll see what I can excavate of you and our history. But everything, really, will be kind of empty, because I can't ask you anymore to tell me the stories about each bit left behind.

Will there ever be a time, I wonder, when part of my heart, part of my attention, won't be turning toward you? When you won't be hiding just beneath the flurry of my marching forward? I am not sure. Things feel so incomplete when I remember you're gone – which is pretty often.

12/4/11

The afternoon sun through the window is so clear and warm that I stand in the middle of the floor and turn my face like a sunflower so I can follow its gentle heat. All I want to do lately is to sink into warmth, to lay everything down, slip into easiness and let go.

I wonder if that's what death is like: a final sinking down. Anything else, a rude interruption when you just want to stop, let all you thought was important fade away, give everything over to that truer, deeper call. Maybe it was like that for you – sitting in your chair, watching out the window, slipping away.

It wasn't easy for me when I was twelve and near drowned at camp – at least not at first. There was fear and thrashing and pushing toward the surface of the dark, churning bay. Then my body gave up, fell down, down. Exquisite, that letting go, that swelling up of something I still can't name, but that, even after so many decades, still stands out crystal-clear. I know I'll fight death when it comes for me, because that's what most living things do – try not to let go – but I am not afraid. The wonder persists.

I guess you got both of those – the fear and the beauty – and now you're on the other side. Are you quiet, there? Are you overcome with joy? Are you part of the ethers that keep breathing the world?

12/5/11

Sun slips through the window, lights up this page and the pale walls where prism rainbows dance. Bodi wanders in to be petted, a little rainbow stretching along his curly back, a hopeful look on his face. Maybe we have a little love room too, this dog and I. We know each other well. My fingers know just how his grizzled curls will feel when I scratch into them, and how he'll smell after a romp in the woods: like mud and pine needles and his own sweet doggie scent. He knows when I'm most likely to give him a snuggle, or when I'm moody and it's best to keep away. We too, have made this thing of love, this tangle of knowing and hoping and expecting to be together.

I've already told him he's not allowed to die.

12/8/11

I wonder how aging was for you. I'm struggling lately with what seem to be the effects of so many years of running ahead of myself and doing what all women do – which is everything, of course. And the leftover exhaustion of taking care of you. My body is tired.

Maybe you can only push a good thing so far before it calls a halt. There are limits. This body I took for granted turns out to be like every other natural thing: lively but tender; both tenacious and fragile. Wanting to be watched over with a fine and gentle eye.

You knew how to take care of yourself. You were careful, ate slowly enough to drive everyone crazy. You walked everywhere you could and did aerobics before anyone knew what it was. You had rules you followed, though not quite religiously. You paid attention.

Somewhere in my early memory bank is the wisp of a story my mother told about you in your sixties, developing some potentially disabling disease. It was something that could have been devastating but that mysteriously went away. I am guessing it wasn't so mysterious. I'm guessing you went after it head-on: found out as much as you could, did research, got advice from Johnny and your doctor cousins, then dug in your heels and fought your way back. Maybe that was the origin of your rugged self-care: attention, rules, moderation. Discipline in everything you did. Those things stood you in good stead.

The effects persisted. Before your cremation, when Esther and Peggy and I sat with your body, laid out plain and simple, swathed in a white blanket, you were so strikingly beautiful we couldn't do anything but stare. "Like the body of a saint," they said. Your face unlined, peaceful, your body slim and straight beneath the drape of cloth.

Now I'm in the odd position of having to pay attention to the body I ignored because I was taking care of yours. A strange doorway into health – but any doorway works, I guess. I hope it's not too late.

12/9/11

You're still a pale, wispy cusp around the edges of everything I do in these busy days. Racing here and there, trying to finish up with school, slinging things together for the Christmas I barely care about so far.

Your pictures on the desk seem a little faded. Maybe that's just the way everything seems to me these days, when I'm so tired and in so much pain. Or maybe the photos are just faded after sitting out for a year or more. Maybe you're slipping farther away. Have I abandoned the love room? Have you?

I'm currently reading a book about the mystical journey of the soul before, during and after death. I'm hoping the book will describe the next year or so and my heart-mind can follow along with you. I am trying to touch you still, hoping there is something there. Someone there. You.

12/10/11

I think you'd be sad to know I'm tired and suffering. I think you'd pray for me and ask questions: who said what about my health, and what's going on. And then you'd tell me to buck up. "People get through things. Life is surprising," you'd say. You'd trust me to figure it out. Still, it would be so much better if you were here.

For the holidays, I'm sending you little mental snapshots of good things happening: Lara, tall and thin and okay; Alison, sunk deep into the happy sweetness of being a mom; Peter, growing and learning and keeping everyone on their toes; Celeste changing some old, hard habits on her own terms. The Vials, still close-knit, living in each other's pockets and hearts. And some Martin kin I'll get to meet up with soon in New Orleans: Lennie and her two daughters, Fred and his sons, and a whole new clutch of cousins. We'll probably be thinking of you.

12/11/11

Very cold today. The pond is a thatch of ice – all shiny, captured light. Everything is quiet.

And then the ducks sail in with a swoop of wings, the tinkling of so many beaks pecking at the new, icy skin of the pond. Their weight sinks the ice a little so they end up standing on water.

How long they'll continue to come, I don't know. I imagine they'll pass by each day to see what's possible, crowd in to the last edge of water before it's all gone. Then they'll let go of whatever hope they held for easier times, and move on.

Will that happen with you and me I wonder? Will you be the pond I can't land on anymore? The place I can't visit?

It's starting to happen already, a little bit at least. Every once in a while I wake up and notice the bubble of emptiness I've been living in, just as it slips off a shoulder. Sometimes it's okay. I find myself thinking that something new is possible, something I couldn't have imagined before. A date? A change I can make in school? A little bit of energy to spare? Or somewhere to go that might take some effort and that's okay?

I'm not sure what it means if I slip out of this bubble of loving you, holding onto you. Will I be leaving you behind? Can I even do that? I thought the love room was just my heart, just the place I'd live in for the rest of my life without you.

It's all so mysterious, this hard fact of you not being here, and the continued existence of this room where we've loved and lived. But it feels like something I can't control, some kind of natural – or even supernatural – process that has to be what it is: the weaving together and coming apart of our hearts.

So I'll keep showing up, keep paying attention. Keep loving you.

12/12/11

Christmas cards. Last year I was stuffing envelopes with a long letter about you and your leave-taking, and a photo of you at 102 and Peter at two – the goings-out and comings-in of our family. Even though you were gone, each letter seemed so chock-full of you.

But now, what is there to write? You're already and still gone. My life stumbles along; I'm not much good for anything, have hardly got the energy for holidays. What is there to say but the emptiness, and who would want to hear about that?

This low place feels like the most natural thing in the world when someone is ripped away. But I miss the playful times, the lighter days.

12/13/11

This past week, the tiny dose of antidepressant I have started to take has lifted me up a bit, and I'm glad. But I want to be careful. Whatever this invisible enclosure has been, I don't really want to set it aside. Even though it's been uncomfortable – weighty and sobering – I want it to unfold as it will. For one thing, it's what I have left of you. But even more, it is real: some law of the universe of coming apart that I don't want to miss. If even animals grieve – if wild elephants have impromptu "funerals" when one of their tribe dies, walking around the lost one in a circle, each taking a turn, trying to nudge the fallen one up, then finally fading off into the trees—who am I to pretend this isn't happening? This low and sunken state, this rarified place?

Are you still there? Am I slipping in and out of you? Does the love room – oh, that world of just the two of us – miss our hands holding on? I have to think it does. Surely the universe must so love, and therefore miss, its children the stars, its snuffed-out sparks of light, any of us who fall.

12/14/11

I seem to be falling apart. I've heard that this happens sometimes to those who have shouldered the mantle of someone else's life, stepped into the details of a loved one's last years and woven them into their own.

My body that has soldiered on for so long is gaining a voice of its own. Is pleading for mercy, for rest, for a halt to anything that isn't light and unencumbered. I'm not sure what to do.

I wonder if you ever experienced the flat-out exhaustion of having lived someone else's life in addition to your own. Maybe not – you were the one who went away. You visited and called and kept in touch, but you didn't shoulder the weight. You weren't standing there in the trenches of trouble. You could always go home, back to your far-away life. And you did.

You stayed planted in your own bright and interesting life. And while I'm glad for that model of how to keep going forward, even when those you love need help, I'm mad at you too. The part of you that was able to sail away might have been the same one that caught me up in your life, let me take on more than I could handle. And now, here I am, more than tired, wrestling with flagging health and nagging pain, no energy to spare.

I feel rattled writing this. If my image of you as the bright, shiny one is more complicated than I wanted to know, are we still okay? Am I bruising the rare and delicate thing we made? Tearing the love room apart? Storming the shores of that lovely place? Probably not – there was always space in our togetherness for truth, even if it was hard, even if it took some work to get there.

And I guess it wasn't all your fault. I seem to have been trained so young to be so good. But you could have helped. You could have been easier. You could have cooperated early, while I still had some liveliness left. You could have listened when I told you I was tired. You could have let me go.

Well...maybe the love room is bigger than I thought and it can hold this too – the anxious mess of my unsettled heart.

12/15/11

I imagine that you are still in some process of being transformed, the many diaphanous layers of your purest self all slipping through each other, all lightening up. I imagine you're still learning, maybe even being newly created, for what are you – or any of us – but flickers of creative mystery anyway? And how could creative mystery not continue to create?

Still, at some point in this, your afterlife, you must finally have to let go. Maybe the sparkly ethers of what made you up will shower over those people and places you loved, a kind of glittery rain that can be soaked up like water by trees, and you'll stay rooted in this world, at least a little.

Buddhists say there is really no separate soul. Everything that lives has free will for its series of lives, but then is re-absorbed into – what? The ethereal creativity of life, I guess, the Buddha-mind.

I'd love to know what you think about this now, from your new perspective. I'll bet you're taking notes. Maybe you'll pass some of what you learn on down to me.

But you know, if you just need to rest, if you're already part of the quivering stuff that keeps making the world, don't worry about getting in touch. You don't owe me anything. And more than answers to questions, I want you to sink into whatever unfolds for you in this, your new adventure.

12/19/11

This morning is brutally cold, just eleven degrees when Bodi and I walk out, and only fourteen when we return. But it has its own beauty. The pond is totally frozen over now, looks like crinkled tin foil. Air bubbles trapped in the ice shift and slide under the inch-thick surface. And suddenly, right beneath the bank where we sit, the muskrat, all spiky hair and speed, shoots ups and surprises us. She is busy, despite the awful cold. No wonder that trappers used to prize muskrat pelts – waterproof and warm. Still, since I've watched so much of muskrat life and diligence, I couldn't wish her dead. No muskrat coat for me!

You might have worn one, though. So many brothers and cousins who hunted – a practical thing to do for that landed tribe, and fashionable at times.

I'm feeling you around pretty often lately – just the sweetening of a moment, a flashing thought, joy spreading out in front of me, flavored of you. Maybe it's the holidays – the time of love flowing over, of family, of remembering what counts. Heart strings tugged in the direction of what's familiar, but could be so easily lost. In this instance, you.

12/21/11

I wonder if I'll look back on this blank, dull time and see it in some way that makes sense: this time of wanting to do nothing; of wanting to turn back instead of forward; of wanting to hear all the stories our people could tell. Of wanting to dip my empty hands back into the past and come up with something rich: pearls of memory, secrets you kept, the smell of that damp, sweet southern air. I need all these like my body needs blood, or water or food. I don't know why.

Oh, how impossible this all is – impossible to turn back, impossible to go forward without you.

12/22/11

I always assumed you'd be gone at some point, that you would just become a trail of vapors, would settle into memory, and I'd move on, happier to have known you, enriched and done. But now I'm wondering: maybe there will always be something left: a thrill; a shiver in the air; a thin, sharp edge; a you-flavored vein of liveliness, pulsing at the center of everything I do. For after all, how could any love be lost?

Will this turning back come to a natural end, or will I have to wrench myself away? Could it be that, in some small but powerful way, our beloved dead take us down with them? Are they like the Sirens near the sea's treacherous shores, teasing us into watery depths where we forget that what we need is air, or what's possible instead of what's already gone? Am I at risk? Is this longing of my heart leading me somewhere I can't really go? Have I forgotten what is real?

But how could I go forward alone?

12/23/11

I remember you saying once, when I felt so emotional about something, that emotions weren't important; that what one could count on, and should follow, was the mind. A sharp and piercing intellect should be the guide of how to steer a life.

But in your final years, when you were fired and forged with all the challenges of aging and life's surprises and disappointments, I saw you change. Your heart took over. You'd cry with love as easily as a child. Joy turned into sweet tears. Standing small and open when I got ready to leave, you'd cry: "Oh, I miss you already" and hug me so fiercely. One hundred years of loving in that heart, that knew how much it stood to lose.

Now, remembering, I am happy and sad and mad, all at once. To think of all those years I was scorched by your fiery tongue, calling out critiques of how I was doing something, often enough to fan the fires of my doubt.

I'm so glad I was there long enough to see your sharp edges soften, to feel the fierce truth of love rise up, to see you sink into that heart that grew so sweet over the years.

12/24/11

Christmas Eve

I'm too tired to write much, but I hope you were around tonight at Alison's to see little Peter, who is so funny and yet so ready to say "no" to what he doesn't want. I think you'd like that in him. He hates having pictures taken—the flash hurts his eyes, he says. He told me it wasn't nice to surprise him, and of course he's right. Being three years old shouldn't be an invitation to invade his privacy, but what's a grandmother to do?

Alison told him to put on his sunglasses, so that's what I have now – pictures of him with an arm raised over his face and his "shades" on. He's a quirky and curious little guy.

And the women: Celeste, here for a visit from Louisiana, and Alison and Lara and me, all together and laughing. I thought of you, your laugh and delight and humor. You would have been right at home.

12/26/11

There's no substitute for you. You are still gone. I am still sad, a little lost. There is no getting around that. Peter won't know you. You won't ever get to lay your fine hand on his big, sweet head. I'm sorry for that. You'd love him to pieces.

12/27/11

Such a busy time. All the hubbub of having visitors and trying to arrange gathering times. You know what that's like, when there are so many people to consider and so many preferences to try to match up. I haven't had time to sit with you, or with your sweet presence in the airy love room .

I've missed that.

On Christmas Day, people who came by stopped at some point in the busyness of the day to pick up one of your photos and comment. Celeste wondered if the man you're leaning against in that faded picture of you – lying on a log, your head in his lap, his arm gentle around you – is our dad in his very young years. But I think the pose is too intimate. Whoever this man is, he's someone you know in a different way than you'd know a brother.

And all of us noted how much Alison looks like your mother - the long, pale face, the slightly turned-down nose, the sober and dignified gaze. Such a rich history in those faces. Yours is more like the Martins than the Vials, I think, except for the eyes – those black, gleaming eyes. Alison has those, and Peter too.

12/29/11

I wonder if you ever felt used up? Was your life ever so busy that you didn't have time to think, but just kept running, trying to keep up with what seemed an endless list of demands? Well, that's where I've been, after helping you, and now I am longing for relief. I want sun and warmth, quiet days and long, dreamy nights, good books in which to get lost. I want lots of lying around watching clouds, watching light move across the walls, letting my own liveliness seep back in so I can fall in love with life again.

I don't know how to make that happen, yet. But I'm taking a vacation next week, so that's a start. Already I can feel a loosening-up as grades are turned in and the list of chores shortens.

Maybe I'll have time to think about you during those unscripted days, to check on the love room, see if it's still intact. Maybe I'll bump into you there.

12/30/11

I guess I'm getting used to you being gone. You're just not here. You've missed one birthday, two Christmases, two Thanksgivings. It's beginning to sink in. Maybe that's okay. Life is moving on.

Still, when I lean over to light the little candle on my desk tonight, so I can sit to write, there is your picture, taken at one hundred years. Your smile, those sparkling eyes. The impossibility sweeps in again. How could a life of being and loving and wrestling just disappear? I don't understand. Or my mind understands, but my body that still surges forward, pulsing with the life we shared, is confused, flummoxed. How can you be gone?

12/31/11

Tonight, instead of going to a party, which would be raucous and fun, I stay home. I want to dig into the piles of photos and letters and stacked-up files ignored for months, and put things up. Throw things out, plow through all that has been waiting for me. So I do.

Near the bottom of one pile, I find the letter I wrote last Christmas and sent to friends and family along with your picture, and Peter's, and a copy of the talk I gave at your funeral in Maryland. The whole unreal reality tumbles over and into me again.

This is still where I am. Everything around me, all the thoughts and plans and work, all the conversations, the holiday rush, happens around the center of this: losing you. You and your absence are still the lynchpin around which all else moves.

1/1/12

On this quiet New Year's Day, I sit at the cold pond, gaze at the snow, the sky, all the sparkles of hidden frost shining in the new sun.

And think about you. No matter what else I am doing, I am missing you, holding onto you, standing at the door of the love room, waiting for you. Maybe this is just how grieving is. Maybe all of us left behind – out of habit and confusion and not knowing what else to do – keep moving forward as if something else mattered, as if everything else were real. Which of course is true. But the still very palpable nearness of you, and the sweet, small enclosure of the love room we share, and the impossible wrenching away of what was so bright and real, still throb at the bottom of my heart.

I am wondering why.

Perhaps I have stumbled upon some shy but piercing truth about death and life: the heart is never done. What we think is real – this journey with its beginnings and endings, its sharp turns and boundaries and walls – is just another breathing in and breathing out, not so far away from that place where you are now. Not so far away from me.

1/3/12

I'm on my way to vacation in Antigua, and then to another gathering of clan in Louisiana. I'll see Lennie for the first time since I was sixteen, and her daughters Kathi and Dorothy, and the usual Hahnville folks. Lara will come too. She'll get to meet them all.

I'm sure we'll talk about you.

It's so hard to explain your real goodness to anyone. There was always your beauty and wit, the laughter, your feistiness and grace. But, more important – the reason I could let you in, count on you – was a certain presence, a dignity. You could stand firm, but you were also willing to be surprised. You could surrender to the unscripted mystery of life that bubbled up and spilled over all around us.

I make you sound like a saint. Maybe you were. Maybe we all are.

1/5/12

Daddy's ninety-seventh birthday – if he were still here. I used to call you on this day, because I knew you were thinking of him, and we'd talk. Together, we were celebrating his coming-in day. Now you're not here and your birthday – which would have been your 104th! – is coming around again. Instead of feeling sad though, I am joyous. Maybe I am coming to some new, resolved, and happy place about having known you, and can let you go. Just let you be.

I wonder how it is for you, and for him, now that you're both gone. Do souls who have moved on to whatever mystery happens next get to see each other? Is our whole gone-family gathered somewhere, glad to have you with them, looking down on who's left here, showering us with little graces from afar? I hope you get to see them all. I hope you get to see my dad. I imagine the two of you, holding onto each other, laughing, telling old stories, warm and airy and light. If he's there with you, will you tell him hello for me?

I haven't come yet to know how much I miss him, even though he's been gone for so long. I don't know why it was easier with you; loving him was just complicated. There were so many layers of longings and loves, all intertwined. He was hidden, obscured, like men were in those days. So he's on my list of people who are gone but still shimmer in my heart, like you. Today, I am loving you both.

1/7/12

I've slipped from being exhausted and writing to your ghost into being a ghost myself.

Maybe invisibility is contagious. Or perhaps those beloveds who have gone away take something with them – a few shades of our liveliness, a little bit of our willingness to be here, some of the courage it takes to hold up our share of the world.

I wonder if this would be different, this passing into living ghost-hood, if I had a life partner who expected me to show up, whose need would tug me back across that line of loss into personhood again.

I am hoping not to spend the rest of my life this way – gloomy and gray – even though right now dull is about all I can manage. Dull is pretty okay. But my friends think I'm boring now. I don't reach out and after a while, they get tired of trying to beckon me back. For me, it's just easier to say no. Still – another twenty or thirty-plus years of this? I think not.

Some part of me will have to shake awake, find a new horizon and make an effort. Reach out beyond what we shared together to see what's left.

But not tonight.

1/9/12

I used to be fun. I used to have fun. Will I ever feel lively again?

1/10/12

After a long day of travel, I stand alone in a motel in the middle of another night, slide the door card through the skinny slot, lug in suitcases and bags. I could be traveling to you. This could be two or three or five years ago. The groove my body knows so well – how to get to you.

1/11/12

Outside the half-open window of the New Orleans airport hotel, I see the land of our people, though earlier generations would be hard-pressed, I think, to recognize it now. They would have to slip beyond the city's snaking byways, pass the frenzied tangle of speed and noise, ease into the watery thickets, follow their noses along scent-trails of mud and mildew to arrive at the quiet fringes of the towns clumped together by kin. Then they might catch on – see familiar faces, hear some remembered names.

Why am I here? What am I trying to find? I don't know yet, but my feet are happy to be landing on this tough, spongy grass, and I want more. I want to trek through the knotted thatch of vines and feral trees at the edge of any field; sniff out the hidden bayous that are dark as a good roux. Sit quietly on some knobby root where the fire ants can't get me; watch egrets rise up out of the grass in front of wandering cows. I want to pop into some cousin's house and hang around for tea. Hear the old stories, tell a few myself.

I don't know why I want these things, but my body has a mind of its own. It keeps turning in this direction. For now, I keep following, waiting to see what happens. Maybe I'll be surprised.

Today, the family reunion. Lots of Vial-Martin DNA, gathering in one spot so we can trace the leftover threads of our people, see how we tangle into each other. I can't wait to see them all.

1/12/12

So much family. I am swamped, in the best of ways, the rivers of love swirling all around.

But a little trouble, too. Keet's house has been sold– that place where several generations of our family were born and raised – where you, Helen, my dad, and all the brothers played out your early years with cousins. The "root of the root," Nanette calls it, now given to someone outside the family, when another cousin might have bought it instead.

The ancient camellia bushes Keet nurtured – some she probably grafted herself – have already been pulled up. A gaping wound, smack in the middle of love and stories. A new story now, of a cousin who didn't let the family know, so part of our history is lost.

Well....there are still the long, open back pastures, space enough to build and settle into a new house, if that's what I wanted to do.

What would you say, Little Honey, about my thoughts of living here? You'd probably ask me why. I wonder, too. But my heart is a jumble of what has left its traces in my genes and dreams. I might have to follow that trail for a while to see where it leads.

1/13/12

A long, fun day with Celeste and Dede, and Nanette and her parents Sunny and Mary Janet. We cracked open the newest version of Cherry Bounce. It smelled like wild cherry and wood. I sampled a sip. You would have loved it.

Nanette asks how it is that Celeste and I never met all these cousins when we were kids. She can't imagine a world without so many kin. And here I have been, wanting more connections for so long, with daughters who grew up thinking they were alone.

1/14/12

I am swimming in family soup. The very air is thick. Did you walk that back pasture, play there with my dad and all the kids? Oh, I so much want to stick my arms into what you had, splash it all over me.

Could I slip backward, sink into what could have been if our little branch of the family had stayed, if my dad hadn't moved away for work, if my mom hadn't felt so insecure with all those close-knit folks? There were certainly times when it would have been a life-saver for me to have that warm, motley crew all around, wrapping my lost kids into their homes and hearts.

But now? I don't know yet. I need to let all these impressions settle, see what makes sense: heart-sense, and head-sense.

Still...all I can think of lately is that land – the wide, flat, winter-bleached fields, the old out-buildings, quiet pastures just beyond the railroad track.

If I were here, maybe I could understand some things – the gifts and the twisty places of our people that showed up in my own life: intelligence and wit; exuberance, and the filmy, depressive depths; passion and sensitivity and the bruise of addiction; the warm, bubbling-up joy that happens when we're together. How did we get to be this way, and where does this fit in my own singular journey of a life?

I am tingling with a little hope. I could be here. I could spread out into this place I loved as a child, when I stood at the closed screen door and looked out. I could open the door, now. I could race into that warmth.

1/15/12

So many waves of belonging, of being swept up in the deep, warm swell of our people.

Lara says it's good for her. After a childhood in the minuscule knot of the three of us, there is this – so many cousins she can't keep them straight, so much history it's impossible to sort out. And the land her family peopled and farmed. She can reach back. She can go to a party and fit right in. She is not lost or unknown. In this motley crew, this overwhelming clot of kin, she belongs. The doors are always open.

And you? You are the way, both forward and back.

1/16/12

Today we all gathered behind Keet's house, traipsed through the big back yard that spread out into fields, talked about Grandma's house that isn't there anymore, but that so many of us loved. The air, always damp, sweet-scented with honeysuckle. We milled around, each of us caught up in our own remembering.

Then we caravanned to the cemetery. Yesterday, Sunny mapped out the graves so we could find everyone. Today, we made our way to you, clambered over tombs until we got to your spot. We brought some of Keet's white camellias from Nanette's yard, set them in a vase, stood quiet for a while. Fred noticed your death date hasn't yet been engraved on the tomb. He said that's because you're probably still around.

Are you dispersing into our people, now? Do you not need me anymore? Do you not need us, because we can do it ourselves, this business of being together?

1/17/12

Home, after the hurry-scurry joy of hugs goodbye, and the busy press of traveling. I unpack your photos. You'd have loved our little reunion. The only thing missing was you.

1/18/12

After the first day of class, I'm still not settled back into my own life without you, without family.

Were you there, in all the excitement of old ties renewed and new ones woven? Were you watching all the young ones of the next generation, suddenly enveloped in our capacious family and the easiness of the South?

Who knows—maybe we'll somehow get more woven into each other over the time we have left. And maybe I'll go south for a while. Maybe, as Nanette suggested, Alison can bring Peter and he'll get to know the place and the stories, and our people will get carried down to yet another generation. We could bring the Martin name back to Hahnville. What a tradition to keep alive, this family all woven together.

For now, I am holding them all in the arms of my heart, where you have been all along.

1/20/12

I am still living in the emptiness you left behind. This one loss seems to have unearthed all the hard things of my past – the grueling, just-getting-by years; the scrabbling single-mom years; the many endings - of parents, places, ways of being. Losing you has triggered all the pain I managed not to grieve before now.

Grieving feels like a hollow cave I may get through but can't walk around; a blind cave and, oddly enough, the only place I want to be.

1/21/12

I don't want to be cheery. I don't want to pretend life interests me. Nothing much does. I don't want to talk with anyone, really, unless the talk swings your way – and words are never enough.

1/22/12

Today I counted up the months of missing you: sixteen so far. They say that two years is a turning point. So, eight more months to go.

But that scares me, too. What would it mean, to be done with this? Only eight more months left of you? And then what—I just pop out of the dark cannon of emptiness? Part of me hopes so. It would be nice to feel light again, to care about something.

And part of me isn't sure. What would I be, then, and what would you be? Gone? A remnant of the love-room tent, fluttering in the wind?

1/23/12

I think you'd remember my friend Mike – you met him at my big house on Upper Ridge Road when you came for a visit. You worried about him because he seemed to be in pain all the time. Ironic that you, in your late 90s, were worrying about someone who was not even half your age. Well, now it seems like he might be dying, or have some terrible disease.

I wish you were here. I could tell you about it, and we could talk. It's hard, loving people when they're suffering. But I guess that's what love is: the heaviness of caring when people are in pain.

I shared some of the love-room letters with Mike recently. He said they made him cry. Today, in an email, he wrote – typing with one finger of his left hand because now he can't use his right – he asked how it was going, writing to you.

Love still cares, even when it suffers. But you'd know that.

1/24/12

This morning the weather has shifted, so there is rain on top of snow, and the warmer air is sweet and smells like spring. Oh, how much I need warmth, and slow days, and rest.

I think that happened to you, too. In Aunt Helen's last year, you took over and stayed, even though you were in you mid-90s. You slept in the same bed because it comforted her, took care of her house, and then settled all her affairs after she died. You came back to your home lugging all her things you didn't want to give away. Then you fell apart. You sat, instead of staying busy, and clutter built up around. You didn't pay bills, didn't file taxes. No one knew just how you really were. So – maybe you were used up, too.

An odd, sad cycle this is: of loving and helping and taking on too much; of getting used up, stepping over the edge of what is really possible, and doing it all anyway. It shouldn't be that way. A whole clutch of people should come out and help. But we were both women alone; took it all on. And here I am now, trying to recover, trying to figure out how to keep up until I can stop.

1/25/12

I'm still trying to keep you alive, bring you back. I wonder how long I'll do that. Tonight, I put up all the photos from the Louisiana trip on the fridge – faces full of smiles and warmth. Yours isn't there, except in Lennie's face, and Fred's and Nanette's – and mine.

Earlier, I read something about the first of the traceable Vials – in Paris and Rouen, Lyon and Mexico, connected, it turns out, to musicians, poets, and politicians, teachers and travelers. Wayne Vial from South Carolina is gathering more of our history, another finger tracing through the rich dust of our genes.

1/28/12

I am thinking about you lately, as I head toward sixty-five – wondering about aging alone. I wonder what that was like for you. Did you worry? Were you sad? Did you sit sometimes with a pile of bills or complicated paperwork, a health concern, or a love lost, a family member's hard time, and wish to share it? Wish for someone to take on part of the worry, explore the possibilities? And what about the joy? Whom did you rush to call when something sweet happened? Who shared those first days of spring, that crazy, lush flowering: family, friends, or some good man?

I wonder about your independence – did it settle, over time, into who you thought you were? Did it close doors on your sweetness – that funny, sensitive place – to do everything yourself for so long? Did a habit become just the way you were?

I can see that in myself. For so long I've had to do everything alone. No one else to tease open those very private places of my heart, infuse the tangle of my thoughts with a little fresh air. Will I, too, grow so used to being by myself that I'll forget how important another perspective can be?

I don't know. I guess I can only pray to stay open to what is best and fresh, deep and possible. I'm having a little ceremony soon, something quiet and mindful, to celebrate sixty-five years of this particular life. What a privilege! Certainly an amazing grace.

I can't imagine what was on your mind, in your heart, at 102. What a wonder that must have been!

1/29/12

I learned to Skype today and it made me think of you. People at computers can call each other, see and talk with one another, right there in the moment, even if they're a world apart. I think you'd love that. I can picture you now – you'd so marvel at the wonders of our world. I'm going to use it to talk with Peter so we can visit every day. I wish you were still here so I could show you. You'd get to see him and talk with him. I think you would have loved that.

1/30/12

This morning, while walking Bodi, I got a little "lift" – a little thrill of excitement about creating a program at work. It was fun for a moment, to feel good, to think of letting myself just run with this possibility and enjoy it instead of seeing it as just another drain on my energy. I could say yes.

But what about you? What about the quiet, dark, low times of leaning toward you? There's something in the quiet, and the waiting, and even in the wrenching loneliness, that I don't want to lose. We are still holding hands. It feels like neither of us wants to let go. If I plunge into this new venture, will I get swept up into the distracted everydayness and lose my way back to you? I don't know.

I guess I'll move slowly. Stop often. Listen, and see how it goes. I know one thing: I won't trade the mystery of this continued togetherness for something interesting to do – not yet, at least.

2/2/12

Are you the reason I don't want to care about anything? Has this great loss, and all the smaller ones through the past few years, made me reluctant to go forward with any kind of excitement, or sense of adventure, or hope? Is my achy heart still lying on the floor of all the love rooms of my life? What would it mean to go alone into whatever else might spin out before me? I don't know yet, but it bears some thinking.

In the meantime, I spent a few hours with Peter today. He is so tall and beautiful, so lively and sweetly shy – and a little wild, and pretty opinionated. Amazing how many firm opinions a three-year-old can have! You'd love to see how his mind works. I imagine you asking him questions to get him to think things through. I imagine you holding his small, soft, busy hand – if you could get him to slow down.

2/4/12

Walking through the snowy woods this morning, up the hill and out into the open field, I meet a couple of women with a dog who plays chase with Bodi over the crusty ground. The women and I chat about our pups and then they walk back into the woods. I could get to know them. Every day, I meet good people I could befriend: intelligent, curious, interesting. But I don't.

Why not? I'm too tired? I'm too busy, overwhelmed? It's too much work? I don't want to be happy? How could I be happy in a world that's empty of you? Would it be a betrayal of all the things I've loved, and lost? Of places where I've laid down my heart, or of those of you who are gone?

How do I paint the world with my own particular colors when all the blushing hues that lit me up have washed away in tears?

2/5/12

My friend Joan tells a story about a man who once worked for her. He cleans wells for a living – climbing down, down, to stand on that hard, mucky bottom, on all the litter accumulated over years, and haul out trash. She asked him how he could stand being one hundred, two hundred feet beneath the surface, in a long tunnel of solid mud, all by himself. He told her that he loved it. "From the bottom of the well," he said, "you see stars." From the bottom of the well, you see stars.

I wonder what it takes to do that – to be able to stand at the bottom of what is dense and dark, and look up to see what would be hidden otherwise, if things were easy, if the way were bright and mild.

Maybe I am finding out. Here I am, in the muck of loss, trying to see what still shines. It used to be you.

2/8/12

I wouldn't have imagined that love could be something resented, but now I know.

This morning I am walking Bodi, whom I love to pieces, who – good thing for him – is adorable and sweet, but takes so much of my time and money. Yesterday, another $300 vet bill for a procedure that might not have worked – already. And he won't walk where I want. And he eats duck poop. And today I have to go home and cook for him because his belly is upset – again. And how much turkey have I cooked – tons! – in the last two years for his sensitive gut? I should be running a turkey farm just to feed my dog! I don't have enough money to keep doing this. How will I ever retire when my dog costs more than I do!?

Once again, love is tugging me along on a leash.

And you: how much of what I feel these days – impossibly tired, unbelievably empty – is you? Love, tying me in knots. Love that couldn't say no. Love that could see what you wanted, what would make you feel at home, and safe. A shared and tender heart, unable to let go. Love – both the blessing and the curse. Would I have quit earlier, if I had foreseen the cost, what I would give up in service of you?

I don't know.

Oh, how can I resent the tangle of care that dragged me down? It turns out that the tie that binds is sometimes a heavy weight, long after the loved one is gone.

2/9/12

Tonight I am getting ready for bed and catch a glimpse of my face in the mirror – too close. All the new lines, all the tiredness, all my years, etched and stark, right there, unavoidable.

Remember the time when I sat working on a basket and you sat watching me? How the sun slipped in the window and settled over us, and you – with your sharp eye and ever-ready tongue – called me over to the glass door where the light was bright, grabbed a mirror, held it up in front of my face, and asked me to look closely at what I could see: my skin, that had loved the sun so much, and whose care had fallen so far down the list of things to do when I was struggling and poor and raising kids alone?

I remember it in slow motion, that moment. You, rising up out of your chair and calling me over. Me, wondering what quirky thing you had noticed outside the window and wanted me to see; a little grumpy at being distracted, a little curious – until you held the glass before my face. Asked what I did to take care of my skin. Until you stood there with your critical eye and your unlined, hundred-year-old skin. And I stopped smiling, stopped being curious. I remember how the smile froze, and how my insides felt – open, and then closed; surprised, then cold. "I know what I look like," I said.

I don't know if I said anything else, but you stopped. I guess you must have seen something else, then, on my face, besides lines: hurt, withdrawal. Maybe you saw the futility of it. Or realized that what you thought of as helpful – a guide to caring for one's skin – was really not so nice. For, after all, what could I do, at that point? Genetics – my mother's face showing up on mine, or decades of sun-worshipping; how could I change that? So you stopped. And we somehow stepped over that moment. I sat down again. You went back to reading, and watching. Maybe you decided that lines weren't the worst things that could show up on my face.

And I have to say, sometime after that, I started to use face cream at night, trying some of those things women do when they begin to age. But it was one of those tricky times, that sharpness that took a while to soften in my heart. One more little way we learned about each other, and limits, and just how far each one of us could go.

Year 2

2/10/12

Walking in the woods alone, over the icy path, ducking bare, drooping branches of the larch, glancing over my shoulder toward the pond that is busy with ducks who have settled this morning into the only open water in this winterscape.

Around me, there are sounds, voices, other trails where people walk and talk. I could be crossing over, sinking into everyday busyness, joining the clamor all around.

But I don't.

This path – the icy, lonely road between worlds – is mine alone; all I really want. If I walk it long enough, you just might show up.

2/12/12

Oh, could I be leaving you behind?

This morning, the sun is up and bright, and even though it's only eight degrees, my body is hopeful. Maybe spring is not so far away. Maybe I can make it through another winter, another year of working, and think ahead about retirement. Maybe I could be happy.

Last night I had friends over for dinner – an impulse I regretted that turned out to be okay. Part of the way through the meal and chatter and laughter, I switched back on again, and it was fun. I was tired afterward – exhausted. But, putting away the dishes and cleaning up, thinking back to talk and warmth, it still felt right; a good thing.

I've decided I have to take steps to poke through the dark and heavy weight that's been pressing me down. I'm lonely. Bodi is not enough. Even the sun, even sitting in this bright window for as long as the light takes to slip around the corner of the house, isn't enough for long.

My heart can't keep stretching out to what has slipped away. I might have to turn toward what is bright and possible, here and alive, new. I need more than a silence that is pregnant with you.

I don't know if the love room will still throb with what has been so real, or how I'll anchor the lively grace of what we were in this life that still wants to bubble up, in and through me, spill out in the joyous rush of my becoming. But I know you'd want this – me, moving forward into what's left of my life. Me, being happy. I want that, too.

2/13/12

I was just getting ready to see you in my dream. But I woke up too soon.

2/14/12

Valentine's Day. I love you. Still. I would have sent you something – a card and a little package of things for your birthday that is only a few days away: chocolates, maybe fruit; certainly flowers. You would have been 104. You were aiming for that.

I gave Peter some small toys for Valentine's Day – zebras, elephants, and horses, and teensy lights he can strap on his fingers. And a book about friendships between unlikely animal species – a cat and a rat, a cheetah and an elephant. The book made me cry. I guess love knows no bounds.

Alison says Peter made them turn off all the house lights so his fingers could shine in the dark. I sure wish you could see him. Maybe you can.

2/15/12

Pearl and pewter and peach colors slip over the frozen pond. The air is warmer, thirty-two degrees. Ducks swoop in to find small puddles of open water. They believe again in warmth. Daylight is longer, now. Spring could be coming soon.

And me? I am taking up the threads of my life, getting ready to weave something new. I might be working on a new basket soon. Pine needles are soaking. A bundle of raffia waits for me to choose colors. It has been a while since I've done that.

And I have the name of a specialist in Boston, a doctor who will check me out to see what could be brewing in my tired body. I am edging toward life again, picking up the strands I laid aside to sit in the darkness with you.

But whatever I create will have to be gentle. There will have to be room for you and the quiet sighs of the love room, whispering all around.

2/17/12

Morning

Tomorrow is your birthday. Don't think that I've forgotten. How will it be, this year, not to have you around? Will I feel low and lost? Even thinking of you in the past tense seems like a betrayal. I can't leave you behind. Some childlike place in me still doesn't understand how this could be real.

Maybe I'll just carry you forever. Maybe every gravesite, for every person, is a kind of collective burial – for all the loved ones gone, as well as for those of us left behind. Where does it ever end, the heart's burdensome joy of not quite letting go?

Maybe we're not meant to let go. Maybe the love room is an integration zone – of then, and now; gone, and here; loss, and love that teaches us something about the everlastingness of care.

That could be true. But I'm not there yet. I hope to be, soon, for both our sakes. I hope my single skin can stretch to hold it all: you gone and me here, and all the joys and struggles. Maybe my whole life will become the love room. I can't wait.

Evening

Could it be you – the reason nothing much has come of this day? Could a cloud of remembering have made it hard to juggle chores that get done half-heartedly, leaving me too exhausted to do anything at all?

I'm still mad that you're gone, angry at the hole you left. I haven't recovered yet.

Did you know what a jolt this would be for me?

2/18/12

Morning

Chores waiting to be done, but all I want on your birthday is to sit in the window's sunny warmth; be quiet so I can hear your whispery voice as you slip in to say hello.

Oh, I sure would like to call you up, hear your voice. But I know you were tired. I guess you were done. So, here I am, celebrating our wondrous days, our ordinary days, our rugged or tiresome days – all of our time together.

Evening

I wish I'd called someone today who loved you, too. It would have felt like having a hand to hold, in this, the empty space of your birthday without you.

I would have baked you a cake if you were here. We could have a little party – for how could the universe ever stop celebrating the birth of any of us, her children, even when we're gone?

Rest gently, Sweet One. Love still holds you up.

2/21/12

On this cold morning, sun comes into the trees, followed by first birds – flickers, juncos, jays, cardinals, nuthatches. I am thinking about warmth, about the future, and how to escape the clutch of cold Maine winters; about Louisiana, and family.

And you; I am wondering again how you were able to leave that tangle of close kin, how you could have been raised in that lush jungle of easy growth, then move away.

I'm wondering, too, about struggles. I heard how much you loved all the family. But did you never tussle, never have to stand your ground, or give over to someone else?

Did loss color the past a brighter hue? Did your heart soften, your memories ease with age? Did knowing you hadn't much time left reveal relationships for what they really were: rough and tender graces, pressing you toward truth?

I guess I am finding some of that myself, with losing you. Your memory is brighter than your everyday self might have been. Only lately do I seem willing to let some not-so-easy things about you rise up to the surface of my thoughts, paint a truer picture. We are none of us perfect, so loving has to bear the diamonds and the dust, as they say.

This morning's walk – cold, uncomfortable, but shiny with the billion frost stars glinting on icy brown soil. Diamonds and dust; grace and work; you and me. Here and gone.

2/23/12

So much is leaning toward spring.

At the pond, ice holds strong despite the rain, but has softened a bit. Trees on the bank lean toward the water. I wonder how far they can tilt before they fall. How far can anything lean toward an edge before its roots tear up and just let go, give over to what can't be stopped?

So far, these trees seem pretty sure. Even the one I sit on, with roots that have risen above the black, pine-needled soil, has no intention, it seems, of wrenching itself toward the end.

You held on, too. Even when things got harder, when so much that you could once do fell away, you had no thoughts of the end. You planted your wiry self and stood firm. When you passed 100, you bumped up your goal a few years: 104, 110. If Moses could be 120, why not you?

And then you fell. "It's just too much," you said. You closed your eyes, and waited. And that was that.

Now, maybe you are a little like the nearby fallen oak that stayed firm for so long and then gave over, fell. Has become, in time, a refuge where turtles rest and herons hunt, a birthing place for what needs shelter to bloom anew – which would be me.

2/24/12

Lighting a candle before bed, I lift matches out of their little black box and glance at your picture. Oh – has this all been real? Have you been truly with me all along? Why don't I feel you now? Could I be losing you? Could I be finally left behind?

Would you whisper to me, please, to let me know? I would really love that.

2/27/12

Diamond moon, sliding through the lace of trees, shining in the window, bringing me to sleep. Do you still love the moon from where you are?

2/28/12

My birthday and, so recently, yours. Another winter, loosening its hold, air softening into spring. And you, still gone, though the truth of your absence is a little less acute.

Are you still between worlds, between memories and the shifting stuff of dreams? Do you still dream from where you are? Maybe all the love rooms in the entire world are the gauzy, glittery stuff that makes up dreams. All those used-to-be people, still pouring care over this, the here-world, even when they're gone. I think that could be true. You, still loving this world, still brought to your knees by the surprising joy of being alive, even though you're not.

Can you be here today, just a little, on this, my birthday? Can you hold my hand, celebrate this, my coming-in day, with me? That would be so sweet. I'll imagine that you're here.

2/29/12

Lately I seem to be waking up; I can see colors. This morning, in the cemetery, there are green, rolling, mossy hills freed from snow. Even the tan beech leaves, still clinging to bare trees, look rich and bright. Still, here I am, without you, and without anyone else, either.

Yesterday I read an article on relationships as a spiritual journey, written by a woman with a strong inclination to be alone, but who loved so much the close press of intimacy in her decades-old marriage: being so well-known; feeling fully accepted for who she is; held, loved, no matter what.

I wonder about my lifelong leaning toward solitude – about the many ways there are to hide, living by myself. About how many sharp edges I've avoided that might have uncovered what was tender and throbbing and rare, and whose nature it is to be shared: my own heart.

Was I filling up my life with you, when I should have been reaching out for some other hand to hold? Were you not just a joyful burden, but a way to avoid looking further than my own blood for warmth?

What have I done?

3/2/12

I know the dead are not enough, that the living have to step back into real time. Our needs can't be met by those who are gone. But what's been happening between us since you left seems so rarefied, remarkable; it still calls my name. I want to keep an ear turned in your direction, let this unfold in its own time.

I hope this waiting for you doesn't get in the way of what might still happen for me, here, in this world. But I can't stop, yet, keeping an eye out for that other place where you might be. Where mysterious graces might still be welling up.

3/3/12

You're supposed to be over. Wasn't 102 years enough? But here I am, still trying to slip out from underneath the dusky blanket of missing you, of having given myself over to your life, and now trying to claim whatever is left of my own.

This see-saw of leaning toward you and then tugging away – I wonder how long it will last?

3/4/12

Shuffling through some of your letters this morning, I find a yellowed, skin-thin note, written in 1942, from Mexico – something about school. Another page in the still-evolving tale of you, showing up in the simplest movements of my days, no matter how finished I think am – or am not. I am still the blank book of our coming apart, still an altar to what has been loved, to all that was possible, and now is not. Except for this – the mystery, finishing up on its own terms.

3/5/12

How much I've left behind – joy, playfulness, fun, lighter times. And how much sadness I've been carrying around. Does this just happen when you lose someone you love? Or is it possible I am carrying not only my sadness, but yours, too? Could you still be sorry that you've left this world? Could you be holding on? Are you thinking of me? I want to understand why this darkness is lingering so long.

Because I need sun. I need lighter times: warmth, laughter, joy. I wonder what else of you I am carrying? What about this habit of being alone?

This morning, I settle into a seat in the near-empty bus on my way to Boston to see the thyroid specialist. Sitting in the quiet, before anyone comes in, the solitariness is so good. I don't know why I crave it; maybe that, too, is you. Maybe it is only in the quietest times that your left-over presence can unfold, reveal itself. The door between worlds can open a bit. That would make sense.

But you needed that, too. I guess we were made of similar stuff. I wonder how you handled the need for solitude and unscripted time, with all the cousins and siblings, all the men who flocked to you. How did that fit together with your sparkly, social self?

3/6/12

Did I love you enough?

Sitting at the frozen pond this morning, watching tin-colored, satiny ice, I wonder about this long, protracted time of our coming apart. Why is it taking so long? Am I trying to make up for something I didn't do? Did I let you know how important you were to me? When my heart was shy or bruised or less than sturdy, did I withhold something that I'm now trying to give? Am I trying to make a whole of something that still feels incomplete?

If you only knew how many of your ways I have taken up, borrowed for my own. You taught me how to live – or, at least, you were one of the signposts upon which I counted. But now, I need to choose a new way that will be mine alone.

I'm still afraid to let go. I still want to lay down my life at the love-room door and say, "Here, take this – a place you can still be, even though you're gone."

But I don't know how long that will serve you, or me. After a while, surely everything has to be laid to rest. And this, my current life, can't find its nourishment in something that is gone. I am still hungry for what is possible, juicy, leaning forward.

3/7/12

This morning I am hopeful, feeling more alive. Bump into a neighbor with another doodle dog; we chat while our pups play, and I walk away happier. I could be slipping out from underneath the grayish blanket of grief.

But I don't want to let go. I don't want to let go. I don't want to let go. Underneath this longing to hang on hides the wrenching truth I don't think I can stand – the impossibility of living without you somewhere close. The crashing waves of loss. The fear of having to go forward in my life, always forging my own path, trying to tell anyone else who I am, when you already knew. You knew me before I knew myself.

3/8/12

Living without you is like walking in the pouring rain without an umbrella. Swimming in a stormy sea. Having only gray days. Nothing I would volunteer to do.

3/9/12

Getting up from my morning "sit" to write and be quiet, I pick up your shawl to straighten it, and instead suddenly press it to my face, wrap myself up in you.

I am a prisoner of love and grief. Will I never be free? I don't want to be free! Oh, how long will I be in this impossible, in-between place? No wonder I never remarried! If losing you, my aunt, is so hard, how would I have survived losing a soulmate? Or – maybe that was you, after all: the sister of my soul? And what can I do, but wait for this to play out as it will?

3/9/12

I think I've been needing people, and didn't even know it.

I am slipping, a little at a time, back into this – the living world. My right hand is reaching forward, into my own time, while my left hand still reaches back.

And the love room? It is still the way-station of our common ground.

3/10/12

This morning we go up through the woods over frozen brown leaves and the remnants of last week's snow. All around the edges of the pond, thin, shiny ice-diamonds have stitched themselves together, so ducks walk on the water's new skin. Bodi and I sit to watch. I am thinking again about you, and grief, and that oneness we weave with another that clings to itself long after the two aren't one.

Which makes me think about Mike – the man I was dating when you visited. You liked him, but were worried about his health. He is one of those people with whom I wove a web that has never quite disappeared. And now, it seems, he might be back; interested, again. Not so afraid of togetherness, or, at least, willing to brave the storm of uncertainty to see what can happen. And me? I'm not so sure. Why would I want to open this heart, which is still trying to get back to you, and let in someone else? Still – I am leaning toward the future, maybe as much as toward you.

I think you'd be happy for me.

3/13/12

Tonight I walked over sidewalks buckled by tree roots that don't know how to be deterred. That push up through black, rocky asphalt to do what they must: plant themselves deep, tunnel through barriers, refuse to be tamed, get what they need – food, water, space, air, light.

I so much want to think you're like the tree roots, undeterred, even by death. You could be out there somewhere. I can't believe you're not.

3/19/12

Here's what I would tell you if you were here: We're having spring a month early, it seems. The robins are back, ducks are nesting at the pond, muskrats slip along the water's edge. Cardinals are singing in the still-bare trees. Last night the spring peepers started up in the almost-eighty-degree warmth.

And I get to see Peter every Saturday; he calls it "Grammy day." His body is so straight and sturdy, his reddish hair thick, big eyes always busy. Yesterday we played in the back yard, picked up twigs and pine cones, sat in the back of his dad's truck to arrange them into piles.

He showed me his new toy tractor and talked to it as if it were alive. It's his buddy, he says. And we had a little disagreement – he wanted to speed off, riding it, but was too close to the street, so I said no, and he said yes, and we went 'round and 'round. I finally told him that I wanted him to be safe, and he gave in. He says I'm his best friend. I sure wish you could know him.

And Celeste and I are going on a long-planned vacation soon, to St. Maarten. Then, in May, I'll be down in Louisiana to see Nanette and Dede and all the other folks.

And after a year of being divorced, Lara is with a new man she really likes, but says it is getting complicated. I am beginning to think that anything real is complicated. Even the lush loveliness of care isn't so easy sometimes: all the differences and edges, what it takes to keep showing up, even when things are hard. Complicated, and humbling – and still worth it.

We were complicated, too, you and me: never exactly matching up, but leaning toward each other with the best of intentions. Even now, we still show up.

3/21/12

First official day of spring! Along with all the earthy things that are thawing and rising up these days, I seem to be coming out of a hole – the one you left. Maybe it's just the warmer weather, or the small increase in thyroid hormones, or the tiny dose of antidepressant I've been taking for a few months now. But I'm feeling better.

Still, my heart is afraid that means I'm leaving you behind.

The remnants of your life and time are still pressing into mine; your life, still woven into me. But something else is calling: the rest of my own life. And love for this, the world where I'm rooted. I still hope, and dream. I still want things – touch, deep talk, play. I want to see Peter grow and learn. I want to see how my daughters fare as they age. I want to be here if they need someone who holds them dear. I have baskets to make, poems to write, maybe a little book about you.

I belong to the continuing mystery of what will happen to the world. I am still unfolding. Maybe you are, too, in some graced and surprising ways I can't understand.

Oh, how much I have loved you. But I still want to be free. How can this all be happening at once?

3/22/12

Two planets in the night sky that have been so close to each other lately – one, large and bright, the other, smaller, shy – are separating now. The big one looks so alone. I wonder if it's sad.

3/23/12

This morning I get lost in the woods, then finally find the road again – something familiar.

You were that – a foundation stone of my interior map. How could you be gone? What will happen to my compass now? It is shifting already, I guess. Louisiana, Peter, spring arriving, writing, and – newly – Mike. And school. These fill some spaces – some of the holes you left. But I wonder what my new anchor will be?

3/24/12

Awake early after a sleep chock-full of dreams. Today, I am going to St. Maarten with Celeste. Sisters, traveling together. You and Helen did that a few times – Jordan, where you rode camels. And Cuba, Paris, Mexico. Oh, the tenacious threads that tie us to those we love slip apart so reluctantly. I am thinking of you. I am breathing love.

3/26/12

The cup of the silvered crescent moon leans toward one big, bright planet, so close, but the smaller one is gone. Oh, where is that tiny, winking spark in all this dark sky? Oh, where are you?

4/3/12

Are you there? Somewhere? I'm having a hard day. Yesterday I got back from vacation, spread out all the banking stuff to work on, tried to figure out how to balance things, how to be prudent so I can afford the rest of my life.

How did you handle all that work by yourself? You must have asked your brothers for help, once in a while. It must have mattered, that you had men to turn to, homey men, comfortable with the ways of the world.

Bodi – my own "man" – wanders in now, shakes his curly head, ears flopping. Cute, good-natured, wide-eyed, staring out the window at a squirrel. Not much good with finances, but good for a snuggle.

Still, I'm feeling displaced, untouched, unknown. I don't want to do everything alone. How often I heard you say that no one should live or die alone. You were hoping not to die by yourself. For what, really, do we have at the end of it all if not a hand to hold, eyes to witness the flicker of our life before it's gone, someone to remember that we were here?

You were here. I remember. But who will remember me?

4/6/12

Lately you feel so thin, insubstantial. Maybe you're just another thing I want to reclaim, and can't. Oh, I want to be back at your grave, bringing spring flowers for you and all the others. I wish your ashes had been scattered onto soil, into the air, the waters. Then you'd be everywhere; I wouldn't have to think of you as being in one spot I can hardly ever visit. I could just breathe you up anytime, anywhere.

I wonder if your death date has been inscribed yet on the headstone. I'll have to call to find out, have to dip my awareness back into that close, warm place that is thick with family – to get the answer, and then do something about it.

Am I missing you? Oh, yes.

4/7/12

This life that has made its home in my body wants to lay itself out, flow in new directions. Play, explore, become what it will.

And the quiet times when I have sat with you? The coarse, muffled truth of loss? Will I miss those, if I follow life instead of sitting with what's gone? Which would be you?

4/8/12

Why are we not trained about grief? Why don't we know how to let go, how to turn back and say, "Oh, how much I loved you. Oh, you were a part of me. Oh, how good it was" – and then lay it all down?

4/10/12

Today was busy: teaching class, paper-grading, a talk with Cathy, dinner, a Bodi walk. Then, for a gasping moment, the raw emptiness of you being (really) gone.

I don't know why it is taking me so long to believe this fact, to live with the emptiness you've left. Maybe death, the final loss, is just so wrenchingly, terribly impossible, it takes a while to settle in, to seep down through the layers of everydayness, of all the ways we cope and move on, to finally rest on the bottom – oh, if there is a bottom! – of the truth.

You must be moving on. I might be, too. Today I felt a little thrill of edging toward relief. The coming of the first summer in almost a decade without too much to do; without taking care of you, or something of yours.

I can feel it coming. I can't wait.

Will that offset the hole you left behind? Probably not. But I might have time, and space, to recover. To rest. To sit with what's left of us. To swim for a while in the so many ways I love this life even though you're not in it anymore.

4/13/12

Thinking of you a little this morning, and endings that seem never to be done. Maybe we just learn to live with losses in their new shape – a little tug at the heart, a slip of memory, stealing into the middle of any ordinary day.

4/17/12

Under the just-setting sun, a pink rain of silky petals from flowering trees settles over everything – fluttering in the air, gathering on streets, in ditches, around the edges of lawns.

They remind me of you – your blend of gentleness and strength. It shows up in all the pictures I walk by every day – in your unstoppable smile, that sparkle, even in a steely glint sometimes.

I can't believe you're gone. I can't believe I am still writing to you. My body, my heart, can't figure this out. Where are you?

It takes only the slightest hint of a memory for my body to conjure up exactly the way you felt, the way the room changed when you walked into it with your curiosity, your smile, your ready wit, your serious self. My body would not be the least bit surprised if you walked in right now (Oh, would that be true!). My mind would have to recompute, but my body would just be happy. Surely each person who is here and then gone must leave a trail that lingers. Surely, all the wisps and shards of leftover care lives neck-and-neck with this, the here-and-now. Surely we each leave a trail of our own flower petals behind.

4/18/12

I rise up out of dreams that sluice off me like water. Outside, the sky is gray with flat, streaky clouds, trees are bright with flowers, doves coo in the first light.

At the pond, the snapping turtle is back. Bubbles roil near the shallows. Her back lifts up out of the water, bumpy as old tree bark. She rises and sinks, notices we are here, slips away.

In the woods, I try to pick a few violets for tea, but the leaves are small and skimpy so I'll have to wait.

Some things take their time – violets, turtles, writing, the love room coming undone; nothing I can rush. I have to learn patience; have to wait for the right, and ample, time. I am afraid, though, that if I don't collect them all – the flaring-up inspirations, the violets flowering – they will slip away.

One more thing that could slip away: the love room. I could be coming out from underneath something big and low. Loss. Missing you. That would be good – and hard.

4/20/12

I remember you in your grumpy times. In your last year, when your helper was edging out everyone but herself, one day you said to me, out of the blue: "It's my money and I'll spend every last cent if I want to!"

Harsh; true, of course, but you had no idea what anything cost, or what you really had, or how much you were spending to have round-the-clock help, or what carrying all the weight of responsibility took from me. That edge in you was sharp, and hard. But we got through, your helper disappeared, you recovered your sweeter self. And now you're gone.

4/23/12

I take your shawl off the back of the chair, straighten it. Even now, I am still taking care of you. I wrap it around myself, bury my face in the black and flowery cloth, sniff up what's left over of you – stand inside this, the cloak of your life, your presence and absence, the way you looked out for me.

Bodi watches from underneath my fluffy pink robe, wondering when I am going to get up out of the chair again, move into the living room, light the small candle, do yoga, pray. And when I'll take off the shawl, hang it back on the yellow rocker that still looks too bare without it.

Probably soon.

4/24/12

In the woods, witch hazel, and beech, and larches are greening up. The ground is nubbled with new sprouts of pipsissewa, blue bead lily, partridgeberry, horsetail, wintergreen. At the pond, fallen maple tree flowers are a crimson litter on the water.

The lushness makes me think of Louisiana – of being in that generous place. And, suddenly, I am near tears. The jungly growth, the heat. Our people. I could be there – go crabbing and crawfishing. We could laugh. We could all talk and tell stories.

I don't know why this means so much.

Is it just my body's longing for what I might have had? Some bright part of me that could have risen up and grown sturdy and strong, but didn't get the right blend of love and light, laughter and belonging, to encourage deep roots, or the faith that I could weather anything? That I could know where home really is?

Is there some visceral poignancy, a magnetic true north (or, in this case, south) that keeps us all leaning toward the place where we grew up, entangled in a mesh of land, place, a tribe? Is this my native self just leaning toward its roots?

And you – am I still leaning toward your slippery spot in that silky tangle of earliest things?

4/26/12

A walk in light rain this morning, past violets, wild strawberry flowers, bluets, and pearly everlasting, all heavy with mist. Rain plinking into dark water at the pond. A kingfisher darting back and forth.

Then home to make these notes of my day-to-day unfoldings in this worse-than-scribbly hand. No one will ever be able (much less want) to read them. I imagine Alison and Lara trying to decipher any of this after I'm gone – flipping through notebooks piled in various corners of the house, looking for their names, trying to trace the thread of their own lives back into the weave of mine. Then giving up in frustration, tossing them out, making a bonfire of what's left of my life.

Remember when you did that in the old Hahnville house? Pulled all the old musical instruments and notebooks from the attic, dragged them outdoors, tossed them into a pile? How fast they flickered and burned. How satisfied you were, to be making a dent in what you saw as mess, while Grandma stood by, quietly mourning what she had wanted to save – all those memories nestled into things left behind.

Holding on. Letting go. None of it easy.

Yesterday I lugged your box of old rugs to an antique store to get an idea of what they were, where they were made, whether I might be able to sell them since I can't use them all. "Vintage Mexican," it turns out, with Mayan images; in good shape, woolen, well made, sixty-plus years old.

The first of your things aired out, explored. It was good. It was hard. It left me, again, tracing back through the threads of your life. Did you buy these in Mexico when you were studying there, or were they

Helen's, part of the many things you sorted and rescued from her place after she died? I don't know, yet; more to track down.

But this work is okay. Maybe I can bear to pore over what you left behind, lay things out, let the questions, and the sadness, and even the irritation, of this job of carrying your life wash over and through me.

I don't know how long I'll be tangled in the leftover room of your life. But I'll keep showing up to do the work, to juggle these remnants of love.

Maybe soon I'll be able to start on the notebooks you left. It will be easier for me to read your careful, disciplined script than it will be for anyone to read this, my own speedy, shorthand scribble. One blessing in the midst of a poignant, stunning chore.

4/30/12

Yesterday, when I was playing with Peter and Alison, leaning over to grab a gift for him out of the messy back seat of my car, I spotted your linens – had to trundle through them to get to what I wanted. Impulsively, I bundled your puffy pink comforter and your rainbow afghan into my arms, held them out to Alison, all rumpled, and said: "Here, do you need a blanket or two? These were Aunt Min's."

I don't know why I did it. I haven't really had time to think of what I wanted to do with them – maybe get them cleaned, put them away in the cedar chest where they could stay safe, unearth them later, think about where they might fit. Do something thoughtful and deliberate.

But, instead, here I was in the parking lot with a rumpled, not-quite-clean armload of you. And Alison said: "Yes! I want them because they're Aunt Min's. It will give me something of hers." She reached across that tarmac and bundled you up, her almost-black eyes sparkling like yours often did. It meant something to her, this unplanned gift. Maybe patching an empty place, a sadness she might have about her son not getting to know you, shoring up whatever threads of connection she felt for you. This was important to her – this bit of your life.

I don't know what stories she will imagine as she sits with them. Maybe she'll think of the small curve of your body tucked into that colorful pile of covers, and snuggle into them herself. Maybe they'll just go into a box she'll shove into a corner until she, too, has time to think about where they should go.

But she needed this, I guess. Maybe we both did. So I am giving your life away. Unexpected, abrupt – and probably a good thing after all. Little bits of you, gracing other lives, filling in some of the holes you left behind.

5/5/12

The thick cloud bank of loss that I've been breathing in, drinking up, chewing, and digesting for these many months of you being gone has been world, sustenance, breath.

And now is shifting. Life is calling me back. I want to do some gentle things – pay attention to the garden, poke fingers into dark damp soil, plant a few seeds. Check to see what might be coming up; be excited at what I find. I want to get to know more people, think about the future, clean up and throw things out, and – who knows – maybe find someone to love.

But what will happen to our love room if I slip back into life? Will it hang, suspended, in the ethers of which it was made, gauzy walls flapping in the winds of emptiness? Will it be a little shrine of your life and mine, intertwined, marking the spot where love stretched across the netherworld of the mysteries of being and not?

Or will the shimmery space of our connection do what every real and natural thing must – lay itself down, come apart, offer itself into the air like the apple blossoms that let go of the branch, drift down in a shower of petals with the promise of another life yet to come, another season of fruiting and feast?

I am guessing that's the truth, for nothing real holds on forever. Everything must give itself over to what can still become.

5/6/12

Outside the window this morning, sun shines, lights up lilac leaves that are swaying in the breeze. Neighborhood lawnmowers start up on the first dry day in a while.

For some reason, this spring day brings me back to those frequent trips to Maryland. I miss your helpers – Esther, Peggy, Rosemary – and you, of course. I miss trains that sped toward you through the backs of so many towns, a blur as we zipped across tracks. And pansies I would pick for you when I arrived. The chapel, where ripe persimmons littered the ground and I could scoop them up. The shop where I could buy blueberry muffins for your breakfast. All those routines, linked together, of my life and yours.

5/12/12

Mother's Day. I am thinking of you – for after all, you were the mother of some part of me: my hope; faith in a future; a spark that might have flickered out if you hadn't been there.

If you were still home, I would call you up to say hello. I might even have sent you a card. I wish I could ask you about your own mother – what was your favorite thing about her. I'm guessing it would have to do with love, and the way she managed the motley brood of you all with such dignity. What would I say about my own mom, if you asked me that? My favorite thing? Her excitement, I guess; the way she loved holidays, and people. Her sense of humor? Playfulness? Spunk? Her love of little things? In fact, why am I not writing to her? Maybe I will.

Today, Alison, Peter, and Lara are coming over, which is sweet, but I am doing all the cooking. Maybe next year they can take me out. I am tired of being the one who holds us all together. And what I really want, anyway, is a little time away from busyness. So – maybe I'll send them off this afternoon and do something quiet and calm.

Tuesday, I'm sure you know, if you still pay attention to my life, I am off to Louisiana again, to see Nanette and Jara, Sunny and Mary Janet and Dede, and whatever other cousins are around. And the land – maybe I'll walk the pastures and go out on the bayou. I can't wait.

5/14/12

On the plane, I try to sink down into a little pocket of my own silence, like you used to do while we all worked and talked around you, your helper's TV programs nattering on and on. You would drift down into your own quiet world. I try to do that now, but the voices swell and pulse. Still, I manage to drift into a not-quite sleep for a while.

5/15/12 *in Louisiana*

What I am doing here, in this flat, green place that feels nothing like my current life? On this very lush land with its rich burbling-up wildness just beneath the genteel order of all things Southern? Am I wanting my people to welcome me in, be so glad to see me, love who I am?

Am I wanting to remake the past, patch together the kindnesses I tasted in small bites at some family gathering? Am I wanting what you must have had, and taken for granted: the nectar of belonging that could feed my hungry heart?

5/16/12

Tonight at Nanette's, some drifts of conversation about you – your sweet self, after the years wore you down and you softened into great age, and your sharper, piercing self that so many of the generation after me remembers. There is no one here who was your peer, of course; they are all gone.

Even with all we can put together of our collective memories, there are still questions, gaps. Some mysteries remain. But who of us can be wholly known, anyway? Whose truth makes it, through time and stories and other people's views, all shiny and clear? Each one of us is a private love room with life, known only from the inside out.

Being here now, with this crowd of friendly family folk, I am mad about what I didn't get so long ago – mad at whatever kept me away from what seems now to have been so possible, so close.

5/17/12

This morning, a pale, melon-colored sky shines through the arch of live oak branches, the lace of Spanish moss. I climb out of bed, step into clothes in (almost) the exact same spot where you, and your mother, and her mother before her, stepped every morning, gazed out across this flat, lush land toward the coming days and years.

Outside, the spicy air is sweet with flowery fragrance. I walk back to find the pasture where land spreads out uninhibited – the land I would have run to when I was young if I had been a different kind of child, less susceptible to being pressed into a proper shape.

Now, so close, I clamber up over the first of chained fences that is cold, wet, and slippery beneath my feet and under bare arms. Maybe I am becoming the girl I would have been – the girl who could have slammed through Keet's screen door, slapped bare feet over that tough, grassy field wet with dew, over the railroad track and into the pasture where the horses and cows and two bulls huff now into the early, rising mist, stare at me with flat, curious faces.

That girl probably would have kept going when the bulls approached, might have trusted herself, and the curious nature of the cows, and crept close, pressed her cool face so carefully to the warm bulk of a neck, breathed in the sweet hay-scented air rising up all around.

But...I am not, quite, that girl. Wary of bulls, I turn around in the mist, head back. Maybe later, when the sun is close and hot and the cows crowd into the shadows for relief, I can try again. I could still become that girl who is not afraid.

5/18/12

Walking under the apricot sky to the river that is churning with current and barges and tug boats, I think again about fear. Our mom's seeped into us early and still surges up sometimes, unexpected and tight. And here, in this lush land, the fear of difference is so prevalent; being "our kind of people" can matter so much. But what about caring, tolerance, curiosity? What about love, even if it's complex?

I wonder what you'd say. We had our differences, but you were intrigued about things that were not your norm. You read about Buddha, Mohammad, and Gandhi. You tried to convince me to return to the faith of our fathers, then softened, were happy that I had found something that worked for me. After all, closing the door on difference is just that – a closed door – and love has a hard time seeping through.

5/19/12

Today Nanette and I went to the cemetery. I brought you flowers, picked from her yard here: ivory magnolias with mauve throats, gardenias, something tall and drooping with blue flowers on a long, thick stem. Orangey lantana, and red penstemon. We lugged them over to the graveyard, dumped out mucky water from the vase, arranged the blossoms and added fresh water. I sat for a minute on your tomb while Nanette wandered over to find her grandparents and great-grandparents, giving me time to sit with you. But, somehow, it still feels wrong, me visiting you with someone else – not private enough. I think about what the other person thinks I should be feeling, and find I feel nothing at all. What there really is, is this: you, reduced to a small box tucked into the corner of this stone slab.

Where are you? Have you sunk back into this land that you knew so well? Maybe you're just wafting in the air all around me with the heat and the flowery perfume.

5/20/12

Waking at 4 a.m. to go fishing with Nanette and Sunny. We take a long, fast ride in the boat through canals and into the shallows of the lake to pick up crab traps. The first early light warms us. We fall in love with the wet, tangled beauty all around – a heron lifting into the sky, alligators rolling up and over near the boat, fish just under the surface. We fend off biting flies, shake crabs from the traps. Green swaths of algae curl away from the boat.

Then Nanette and her dad take photos together, entranced with the first sun shining through dew-heavy spider webs at the bayou's edge. Watching them, I am both happy and sad. What would it have been like, to have a father for as long as Nanette has had Sunny? Still – here I am now, doing what my own dad might have done. I am slipping back through the doorway of family and the places he knew, to get what I thought I had lost.

And you – did you prowl these bayous with your brothers, cousins, some young boy who was smitten with you? Did you paddle and fish, gather crabs with your father, anchor your own roots in this wet, black muck before you pulled up to fly away?

5/21/12

This morning, under the lightening sky, I make it down to the Vial canal – the boundary of this place where seven generations of Vials and several of Martins have lived. It is narrow, clogged with purple water hyacinths. Cattle come close and then scatter. Mist rises up all around.

I am being that girl after all, it seems. I am walking on holy ground, breathing up spicy air that is fragrant with dew, cow dung, magnolias, honeysuckle and sweet olive. I breathe up family. I breathe up memories and stories and dreams. I walk on history, thick as thatch, lively as blood.

Overhead, soft curls of Spanish moss hang. I want to bring some to Peter. If he comes some day, we can climb over the gates. We can pet the butterscotch horse at the first fence. She will snuffle our hands. She can eat carrots from our open palms.

For now, I can't inhale deeply enough to take in everything I want, everything I thought I'd never have, and don't want now to lose.

Are you watching me? Are you noticing that I am coming back, dipping my dried-up roots into this, the moist soil of our family? I wish you were here.

5/22/12

This morning, I step out – one last time – into the close, sweet, already-warm air, into the flowery perfumes of damp, dark soil, so many blossoming plants, the nearby river. Then drive away from the welcome of this big, lively, close-at-hand clan and am surprised by tears. I have managed to step backward into what I longed for, all those childhood years ago.

I don't know why I needed this, but it feels so good. This is my place, if I want it. These are my people. I have found what I glimpsed, so long ago, and the door is still open. Maybe it was never closed. Maybe I just turned away before I could soak up what I needed. Maybe I was so weak, so hungry, I didn't have the strength to say yes, and to let it in. The casual neglect of a booze-centered home, then the wreck of an early marriage to that mean thief of my heart, might have left me gasping and frail.

Somehow, you've become the key to the door back into what was once possible, and where I am now. It is a warm and gentling way, this new road, peopled with the very familiar faces of our kin.

What will I do about all the pieces of me that I don't think will fit in this new place? Me, a dyed-in-the-wool liberal in conservative territory, preferring the truth to what sounds polite; a non-drinker with the leftover scars of growing up in an alcohol-afflicted home; a woman still loving the crisp, sometimes abrupt, clip of Northeastern speech and practical values.

I don't know how it will work, this new coming to ground, but I am on my way to finding out.

5/23/12

Back in Maine, reading a book about Louisiana and the at-risk coast, I am tugged again in that direction. My body remembers what it came from, keeps leaning back. I'm not sure why. That luxurious, tangled place – did it pull on you, too, once you were gone?

5/24/12

A shorter, but good walk this morning in the lushness – a hazy mist, sixty degrees, my body leaning forward into the coming warmth, into the green.

At the pond, one big turtle slips through the tea-colored water, moves toward the log. Mist rises up from the pond so the air is damp, my hair heavy with tiny droplets.

Some thoughts of you, and family, and wishing there had been time to talk with Nanette's father Sunny about you. He's the last of those who can remember you or anything else about that close knot of family from so many years ago. You were twenty though when he was born. I wonder how much he would have picked up from you in your short visits home. Still, he is a pretty astute observer. He could at least give me a Sunny-flavored taste of you.

He talked about Uncle Major, said he always knew where to find him: at the nearest bar, having a rip-roaring time. Funny, how different my childhood memory is of my dad's next-oldest brother – quiet, easy to be around because he didn't chatter on and on. I could feel pretty comfortable just riding in the car with him when he ran a few work errands.

I am missing Hahnville today – the back pasture, the haze of mist lifting up from fields under the big orange sun.

5/25/12

How odd and complicated it is to love so hard, so much, and yet feel so happy to be free.

This summer now stands empty before me, after so many years chock-full of working for you. Even though it is sad not to be heading toward you, worrying over you, wondering what is right to do and how to do it all, this unscripted time is good. And mine; a very new thing.

I don't know how much of you will still cling to what you left behind. But maybe getting through your leftover things will help me to shimmy out from under the sweet, sad weight of carrying you.

Will you wait with me in this next stage of our adventure? Do you keep an eye out, a heart still turned in my direction? I am pretty sure that's true.

5/30/12

A walk this morning through wet woods to the pond where a snapping turtle works at her unlikely nest in a woodchip pile. Frogs plop into water as we pass, the kingfisher dives nearby. Six wild geese peck through sodden grass for bugs, murmuring to themselves.

I pass headstones in the graveyard on the way home, and remember Rubin's call from the church in Hahnville. He has set in motion the work of getting your death date engraved. Working on that from a distance has been a challenge, but at least the process is underway.

I wonder if it will make a difference, having you "officially" gone – written, really, in concrete. Will it close some final door, for you or for me? Could it be that you get to float around in the ethers of that peculiar place, as long as the last date hasn't been declared? Will stamping your leaving-day take away some ticket of privilege you have to still be among us? Will it matter at all to you, wherever you are?

Maybe it will be a true and final chance for you to rest – one more step of returning to the impossible mysteries of being and not-being, the end of your share of the Unspeakable Loveliness. But will it seal the doors, finally, of the love room? Will I be kept out, then?

Maybe I need to be released. Maybe you do, too. And maybe that date, engraved, will close the long, vibrant chapter of your life, and leave you free. I may never know. But I'll keep showing up to find out what I can of where you are. Maybe little wisps of you will still surround me. That could be true.

6/1/12

This morning, the woods floor is still mucky in spots. We walk past early honeysuckle with scarlet fruit, first flowers of maple-leaf viburnum, a tall lady slipper that has been a bright spot along the trail for a week or more – and stop. Though its ridged, green leaves are still intact, the perfect orchid flower has been snipped clean off by some passing (and ignorant) enthusiast. I have a little mental tirade about conservation and the lady slipper, now unable to seed itself.

All of which makes me think of you: your solitary journey, never bearing fruit. I wonder if that hurt. I wonder if you went through those early and then middle years longing for what so many women do – your body aching to turn itself inside-out, to share not just your mind, your heart, your joy, that sharp insight, but the stuff of your own flesh into a new being, as your mother had done six times. Is that why you didn't? So many siblings, wriggling all together under the small umbrella of her arms? Or was it just not the right man, at the right time? Did you find something of being a mother in keeping an eye out for me? Were nieces and nephews enough? Or was it just the truth of the times, the choices a woman had to make: a career or a family?

I wonder at what point you just gave up.

6/2/12

A flurry of early chores: feeding Bodi, texting to figure out what the daughters and I are doing for Alison's birthday (here for omelets, me cooking). Then a walk to the pond. At the water's edge, the mama mallard sails over from the tiny island with her chicks trailing behind – only two left out of the original eleven. They are spunky, busy, scrabbling for seed. I am happy to see them, though sad for the nine chicks lost. Another big bite out of possibility. How sturdy a tender heart has to be: How strong the turtle's; how resilient the mallard mother's; how tenacious my own.

Both tender and strong, that lynchpin of survival. You had that. The tenderness bubbled up toward the end. I am so happy I got to see the gentle opening, those tears of both joy and sadness, the vulnerability. That final surrender. You did it all.

6/5/12

What will my life be if it isn't juggling some part of yours? Will I always be reacting to you, pulled along, sometimes so willingly, in the wake you left behind? Was it true, always, from the time I've known you? Was I a kind of homeless child until I saw your spark of light in the murky confusion of those early years? Have I always been following you?

And what would it mean to move on? What if I go to the storage unit, pore over what you left and hang your mirror somewhere on my walls? What if I start using your things, or giving them away, or leaf through your letters one box at a time? Will you disappear, once and for all? Will you come undone?

I am tempted to absorb you – sniff up the dust on the old box lids, breathe those holy specks of what's left of you deep into my lungs, let them mix with this, my own breath, so you can never be gone. Then, my body that continues on and on will be the living love room – my life, the shrine to yours.

I know this is weird. I should be letting go. I have a life that isn't you, or yours. But how, oh, how, do we ever really finish with someone we've lost? And do I even want to?

Helen, my friend who is turning eighty soon, and who knows what it is to lose love, says that we can never let go. Our beloveds become part of what makes us up. So this, my beating heart, will be the altar, the shrine, the flickering flame that testifies to you, who were here, and now are not; who shone through the darkness, and now rests somewhere in the shadowy world of the afterlife.

I hesitate to write these words, but how else can I say what seems to be, really, unspeakable? The End?

6/9/12

I'm visiting Eleanor's camp, near Rockland. At Owl's Head Beach, where the tide has just swept out, sand is cool and packed down. The warm air smells like fish and water and salt. The noise of children playing and families gathering lifts up all around me.

Last year when I was here, I was still working on your stuff. I talked with Eleanor about aging, and loss, and letting go. This year, you are farther away, I guess. It will be curious and sad to be here in this very familiar place without your work at the edges of everything I do.

6/11/12

This early morning, layers of owl conversation wrap all around the camp, raspy and haunting.

Trees shift and shiver in the wind. The sky is clotted with clouds. Wild sounds rise up in the air: fish plopping back into water; bullfrogs twanging; crinkled, tin-colored water licking at the shore.

Still, I am feeling kind of blah. Wondering again about you, and me, and our lingering togetherness. How much of my intimacy of connection is still pouring out in your direction, while my "real," ongoing relationships feel kind of vague, not quite satisfying? Maybe

I should be writing letters, saying real things, to those people who are still here – whose love and thoughts and actions still make up the pulse of my here-and-now.

Maybe my love room with life should be crowded, should be facing toward what is still warm. The tender tangles of what it takes to be together with someone, deeply, can certainly only be carried out here, in this everyday play of being.

Apparently I am a kind of coward – turning toward what is easier (though still so hard). For, after all, our connection is only peopled now with me: my thoughts, feelings, questions. You can't answer back. You can't challenge me on what might not be so true, or only one side of our story. And even though I do feel you sometimes in sweet, quiet ways, I wonder lately who I am really writing to – or for.

Is this love room with you a great grace, or just another place to hide?

I want this to be easier. I want you back. I want things to be the same. I want the warmth you were from the time I was born. I want our story that keeps shifting, getting shinier. I want the me I hope you knew.

But I guess that's not possible. Who we were through all those years – we can't return to that. The room of my own life has continued to grow, to ripen, to generate new things. I am not sure I can do that with you, now. I need to do it with other people, even if it's hard.

6/13/12

At Eleanor's for tea. She is still in her jammies and robe against the chill. We chat while dogs roll around on the floor, playing. Eleanor invites me for supper. I feel like I should give her some time, but try to push our getting together into the end of this day that I am saving for quiet, for writing and editing and, mostly, for being alone. For restorative time, enfolded in the great green silence, the lush empty wildness just being itself, all around the camp. For healing what is left of the tiredness of carrying you in the midst of an already-busy life in this often-frenzied world.

6/18/12

Back in Portland, I have an at-home day filled with little chores and joys: cleaning the car; eating the first of the sugar snap peas out-of-hand; watering gardens; and sitting in the sun for a while.

And now, making notes, charting small details of my life. You did this, too. Your notes to yourself were chock-full of so many things: what you'd done on any particular day; who had called or stopped by; things you'd read; little inspirations; drafts of letters you'd sent; a scrap of a poem. And self-admonishments: such a sharp, critical eye you kept on yourself. What a war you waged, trying to herd whatever small faults you found back into some kind of forgivable order. You gathered them up, your every-days, all captured in that fine hand.

One more way we loved the world together.

6/20/12

Tonight I am washing dishes and – for no apparent reason at all – am suddenly filled with a sad, sweet weight of losses: my dad, and mom, and you; places gone and friends far away; chances passed by. Oh, how many loves we lay down on the altar of living and losing and moving on.

6/21/12

On this, the first whole day of summer, we walk through the woods in sticky heat – eighty degrees at 7 a.m. Bodi pants and looks for the shadiest spots to walk. The sweet heat settles into my bones.

At the pond, bullfrogs hang in the water, ripples swinging out around them in the silvery, motionless mirror of the pond. But, despite today's beauties, I can't settle. Now that this summer spreads out all around me, and I don't have much of your work to do, I want people. I need to be known. I need to talk and listen, do new things. I want to be touched, to have fun, to be silly, or serious, or just plain boring. To be together. With.

I talked with you once about loneliness, mentioned that my mom sounded really lonely when I phoned her, but you pooh-poohed my concern. "Ninety percent of all the people in the world are lonely," you said. I am guessing you knew loneliness well, having lived alone for all your adult life. I wonder how you managed, what you learned about yourself, how you settled into satisfaction. Maybe you reached out, made sure you were linked, arm in arm, face to face, with your special folk. Still, in the end, there was only you.

I don't know what that means for me. I do know that this ache of disconnect is hard. You were my "person," and now you're gone.

6/26/12

I get up out of the rocking chair and race to the living room to get something. By the time I've reached the hallway, the thought is gone. I stand still; try to pluck the memory out of my totally blank brain. Turn around, go back, as if entering the room I left – the space where I was when the impulse hit – will help me to snatch that thought right out of the air. And it works: the bird book, to look up night herons, and figure out if that's what I saw on this morning's visit to the pond.

I've read that stepping back to where you were when the original thought came will help to recapture it. Memory, they say, can be triggered by those surroundings, as if the ethers of our thoughts, the electric currents flowing up and out of our body-mind, still linger in the air. We can re-enter what we left behind, a kind of love room, I guess, with the particular moment.

The beginning of this particular story? At the pond this morning, just where the path turns into the muddy bank of the water, a dark heron stands in the shallows, wide, pale-gray wings drooping; its black-crowned head turned toward me, eyes steady, alert.

I step closer. It moves, drags wings up out of the water, tries to fly. Then stumbles, settles back into the pond; sips up water with that long, pointed beak; keeps an eye on me. Is obviously hurt.

So, instead of sitting, Bodi and I race out of the woods, up the trail toward the cemetery garage, where the groundsmen stand bantering, having morning coffee and cigarettes on this cool, early day. I pass along details: where the heron is, that it needs to be rescued. He will contact someone, the crew boss says, tell the game warden, who will be there later in the day. Still, my head buzzes with concerns – and with heron prayers.

Which takes me back to you, and the things that linger after they're gone. If even my momentary thoughts can hang in the air after I've left the room, why not lives that lasted over one hundred years? Why not the loves and ethers of a whole, long, hearty life? And if one life can linger, why not two, intertwined? Why not all beloveds torn apart?

Now, after so many busy details of trying to help the heron, I am wishing there had been time to sit at the pond, to just be still and quiet, and to rest. But how could I be still and contemplate beauty, when beauty was right next to me, struggling and hurt? So – this day will have to get by on the light rain pattering now outside the window, on the happy call from the bird rescue squad saying that the heron has been taken in for care. And, of course, on more musing about you.

7/1/12

Yesterday I got an email from Nanette, who says it is one hundred degrees in Hahnville and the air is stifling. No break coming anytime soon. You would remember those days, when you didn't want to move, just find a shaded spot and wait out that mean heat.

They went out on the bayous and down to the lake to pull up crab traps. The banks were tangled and lush with so many flowering things. I would have loved it, she said. There were ninety crabs in the traps that had been left for the few days of an impending tropical storm. Dede was happy – she so loves crabs.

It makes me long to be there, to see the bayous all in flower, and to talk with Sunny about you. I want to do that soon. It would be worth braving the heat for those good things.

7/3/12

Tonight, I blow out the candle on the little bedroom altar where your photo stands. Oh, I don't want to accept what I already know: You're not here.

7/4/12

Evaporated milk. I am not thinking about you at all, just pouring hot water over a tea bag, blowing a little air into the clogged opening in the can so the milk can flow, then sloshing a stream of it into my mug. And there you are again. Still.

I've been using it since you've been gone, this fatty treat, like you did. It is rich, poignant: a small river of loss and joy, poured into my daily cup.

7/6/12

Driving to the beach on this hot, sticky morning, I heard on the radio a woman scientist say the seas are dying. Ninety percent of the ocean mammals gone. Coral reefs, thirty percent gone. Signal species, she called them: things that announce the state of the world through their own lives and deaths. Maybe you were that for me – one of the markers of a time, disappearing.

Listening to her, I was swamped with a primal sadness. Every breath hurts.

I think so much these days about the ending of things, am heavy with care. I don't know what to do. Don't know how to bear all this weight of sadness and rage, and guilt for what we've trampled. I don't think I can stand it all.

What about that shimmering, heart-breaking-open joy that wells up so easily in me at watching the booming, floating frogs? The night heron sailing up out of the brush and settling in high trees? The purple fields of clover? Frilly catalpa blossoms raining down in the first summer storm? How does that all stand side-by-side with the awful news – that isn't news at all, of course, but just enough accumulation of struggle, threats, obituaries, to finally pierce through our not-wanting-to-know? To tip the scale of denial into awareness?

Now, as I am writing, Bodi jumps up on the bed, wanting to be near me. He is happy – fed, napped; not perfect, but okay. We press our heads together. I kiss his fluffy, cream-colored paws that smell like mud and dewy dampness.

Bodi doesn't believe in the end of the world. He believes in now. I wonder, though; I imagine that he, in his half-wild heart, is strung together with all those other shimmering pearls of life – frogs and elephants, whales and coral reefs and polar bears, sundew in the sandy bogs, and herons hunting at the pond. I believe he knows, in his doggie heart, that things are not so sure anymore. But – here he is anyway. He has to trust his life.

What would you say about all this, I wonder. Did some part of you know where things were heading? You saw the world become complicated, the lives of those you loved get harried and hard. I think you wondered about that.

I wonder where you would have put your fire, your care and time, if you had lived longer, if these uncertain times had happened during your lifetime. I'm wondering where to put mine. In learning more, I guess; finding ways to help, and, oddly, in joy.

I don't know if it really matters to the oak tree I lean against every morning at the pond that I cherish it, or to the turtles that I wonder about them, or to the heron that I care he was wounded and now has flown away. But I have to think it does.

7/9/12

This time last year I was wrapping things up – finishing up your accounts, grinding through long-winded chats with the lawyer or with family members awaiting word or checks.

It feels strange now to have none of that to do – maybe a reason I've been feeling unplugged and exhausted lately; adrift. Lots to do but nothing, really, to do. I want to sit in the sun at the side of a quiet pond for a long time, letting in the gentle warmth. Sink down into a stillness that is restful, that expects nothing from me. I want to let go.

What else is there to say? You've gone and left me with this – the truth. The job of moving on. I don't know if I'm ready. I don't know if I can do it – or want to.

I am still breathing you, though. It helps if I imagine that. Along with the heady, sweet scent of milkweed blooming around the edges of the fields, in the damp, hot air of this midsummer, I am breathing you.

7/16/12

I want to go to Maryland, to see your place again, and your people – Peggy, Esther, Rosemary. I want to reminisce, to link arms with those who wrapped their own arms around you when you were slipping away. We were, all together, a chain of caring, holding up your life. I am missing them. There's no answer to that, no real relief.

But one good thing – yesterday I got to see Peter. He came over, dressed in his Sponge Bob underpants and his green Hulk sneakers and nothing else. He likes white foods, wanted me to fix him a white omelet (no yolks). And when we ran to the little corner store for ice cream and I asked him what kind he liked, he said "white." He's a vanilla guy, so far. In terms of food, at least, he's a purist. You would love him to pieces.

7/17/12

A hot, sticky walk to the pond to watch frogs, then home, sunk low again with loss. I can't look at the frogs hanging in the cloudy waters without thinking that they're at risk. What about the sad list of all that is wounded, suffering, gone? How can I look out and see anything but threat?

And what about our young people, who may never see butterflies or whales? Who surely will never know what silence is? Who will grow up afraid of the sun?

In the talk I listened to last week about the state of the oceans and the world, one woman talked about aging – how getting older is always hard because you are losing so many things: abilities, options, friends, family, a place where you've lived for so long. We are the first generation, she said, that is also losing the planet – the very earth out of which we were born. Everything we've known as the surest home – the loveliness, all the twittering, creaking, scritching, fluty, wild songs that made up the background of our whole time here – going away.

How can I know all these hard things and still leave the door of my heart open? How do I fall in love, over and over, with the life that spreads out in front of me, still rich with possibility, when there is so much to lose? How can I love frogs and bees, whales, dolphins, oceans and air, dark soil and wild herbs, when so much is wounded? And you: How can I love life without you in it? How can I thrill with the moving forward of my own life when yours is fading away?

Still...this morning I watched a mother cardinal sweep out of the underbrush where her babies were hidden, slip over the dewy lawn to perch in the shadows. My mind was crowded with heavy, sad thoughts. Then my eye caught on the curve of her wing, where her dusky breast slips toward red, and fell in love. I don't know where it came from, that wonder, that startling truth, but it was enough. Undaunted by numbers, statistics, obituaries, fear, it was everything, and enough. The wonder at the heart of all things still lingers, surely, even though you're gone. Even though everything could be gone.

7/24/12

On retreat in Santa Fe, awake at 5 a.m. to an inky sky, two pearl-bright planets hovering at the dark horizon. I walk up the rosy, craggy-stone mountain in the cool, dry air to a parched streambed. A little trickle of water is all that's left of what used to be a pounding, gushing river, nourishing this rare and lovely desert land.

I watch hummingbirds zoom into that small bit of water, am fanned by tiny wings. I think of you: how much you might have liked this place; how you might have braved, in your younger years, the bear tracks, the scrabbled trail, to sit here where the cool, pink mountains fold into themselves, and the tiny, bright birds flicker.

I must be missing you.

8/1/12

Recently, my friend Beverly talked about a memoir she's been writing and how, now that her mother has died, she is realizing that parts of it are not her story at all. It's her mother's story, instead, that welled up and spilled over into Bev's early life.

It makes me wonder about you, and me, and my curiosity about that long swell of family that spilled into us and has come to rest, here, in the moving forward of my own life. How much of what I've leaned toward has been what you might have done? Whose voice, I wonder, has relayed this story? Was there a tale you would have told, and have I been telling it instead?

You said you wanted to write about your impish childhood, that happy passel of kids. "Yellow Cotton Underdrawers" was your title. Six children in a family that was culture-rich, land-rich, and money-poor, wearing plain, un-dyed, muslin underwear made by your mother. So climbing trees, scampering onto ladders, chasing each other around, anytime you looked up, that's what you saw. What an image that conjures up – skinned knees, bursting laughter, a tired, hot tangle of children stuck in a tree.

Even now, it is a tiny taste of your story that I would gobble up; spoon up bites if I could somehow taste the flavors of my beginnings.

I don't know if that answers the question of whose story I've been writing. Maybe it's a joint effort, our two lives nestled into each other; me, holding the pen because you can't anymore. Is that okay? Does that somehow make it inauthentic, this tale of being together and coming apart? Maybe no story stands alone. No life or death tale goes untouched by all those others that swam through and around us, moistening the soil of our roots.

8/2/12

Mike recently loaned me a book about the South, a scholarly tome covering many dimensions of what it means to be "Southern" – geography, how people identify themselves, what makes anyone think it's the best place to be. Culture, leisure time, family, food, religious affiliation, politics. Pretty interesting. One thing they left out, though: land; place; and the way that figures into how we're formed.

I keep feeling so drawn back, to the people, and to that flat, heavy soil, the wide sky, waterways, all the creeping, buzzing, and throbbing wild things on the edges of even citified places.

A friend said recently, when I mentioned this, that she thought my quirkiness was Southern: the love of plants, herbs, and wild animals; how I need to plunk myself down in a spot, walk all around, lie on the ground, plant my own roots; how I have such a hard time leaving anywhere I live. She associates those habits and hungers, she said, with being particularly Southern.

Is there something about the heat, the lavish, wild abundance that gets under the skin and doesn't let go? Is that why I have such a hard time losing places, people, you? I think of those qualities as characteristic of indigenous peoples: always linked to, identified with, the place where they sprouted up. That makes me want to visit soon. I don't know why it might matter. But it's always good, I think, to know more about how we're made, what influences how we turn out.

8/3/12

I stretch out on the living room floor, feel achy muscles, think that maybe I could bring myself to sign up for a yoga class soon. So far, despite all the ways the "weather system" of grief and grayness has lightened in the last few months, it is still a place within which I am living: the loss, the emptiness, the shadowy weight of you being gone.

Could I really be ready, almost, to slip a leg out, an arm; to stretch in a direction that would be living instead of hunkering down at the altar of loss?

8/4/12

A shorter walk through the woods this morning, over a little trail and then up to the road. As we're leaving the path, a loud crash shakes the ground—a tree falling, suddenly. A whole, huge life, interrupted.

I want to go back and see, but have no time. Still, it is on my mind, that tree, so long alive, then – suddenly – gone. It could be you. You could be the tree falling in the woods that nobody hears. Except that I did. And I wanted to go back.

Is this the way it always is for those who lose someone? Compounded by the fact that you were the last of the elders in our clan? The last of those bones and skin I could press against that were part of my dad? Are my organs, my bones, lonely? Is loss visceral? Do all my cells suffer? Is my body still bent low, even as my mind, my intentions, creep forward?

8/6/12

At the pond, turtles bubble by under the water, frogs hang in the shallows. Air is thick and sticky, blackberries at the brushy trail ripe and tasty, my fingers stained purple after eating a few.

Is all this happening inside the love room bubble? Are you still paying attention to what I do, siphoning off little tastes? Am I still loving this world, not just for myself, but for you, too?

8/11/12

Surely the air is made up of multiple layers of grief: of all the people and things we lose. Of capacities, and ways of seeing ourselves. They must shift and rearrange themselves around us all the time. Is it possible, really, to do anything fresh, anything that isn't wrapped in the gauzy, not-quite-palpable skin of what was, as we go about our supposedly brand-new days?

I saw that happen to you, saw the ways you thought of yourself – all tidy and well-packaged – have to shift, crumble, change. Each time, you'd protest, be surprised and then make a new story, a new way of seeing yourself. Once you told me that you were shocked every time you looked in the mirror. You felt, inside, exactly like you had at twenty-eight or thirty. The face you saw reflected was such a surprise. But you were nothing if not adaptable, resilient. Almost to the end, your expectations could shift. "Oh, driving is not so easy anymore. Oh, walking is hard. Oh, my mind can't pull things back so readily. Oh, I can't put together what my eyes are seeing to make any sense." And, finally: "Oh, it's all too much."

Then you let go.

8/13/12

At the Owl's Head beach again, I lie on the sand near an old man who sits alone, nodding off, at the end of a long line of abandoned chairs for family who are playing down in the cold water. He wakes, pulls the big beach towel up over his bare knees, his tee-shirted shoulders, chilled even in this seventy-degree summer sun.

I wish you were here. I wish I could do something for you, one more time: wrap a blanket around your pale ankles, bring you something sweet to eat, or just be quiet while you sighed in and out of sleep.

8/15/12

This morning, Eleanor serves up tea and troubles. She is overwhelmed with stuff – rooms and rooms of stuff; treasures she collected over decades, each piece with its own story. All the things she agreed to store for other people, twenty-plus years ago, are still there, tucked into some corner of some room on some floor of the house or shop or barn. She tells how each tidily dusted pile got there, and why the owner has not yet claimed it. She is the tender of leftover stuff!

My own piles of stuff at home, so much of it yours, are still waiting to be pored over, sorted through. Maybe some of it is other people's stuff you couldn't give away: Helen's, Johnny's, Major's...all now mine.

8/16/12

Today – some catching up to do, school prep, banking, info about retirement. I'm starting to get excited about having time for creative work that doesn't feel like work at all. I feel light and lifted up, just imagining it.

I wish I could ask you about your own transition. You worked until age seventy and then left reluctantly. You so loved teaching, stayed in your little apartment on the edge of the campus when you retired so you could be surrounded by the playfulness and ideas, and even the noise, of students. You wouldn't have it any other way. Maybe it reminded you of growing up, all those young bodies jostling around, raucous and bright.

Some of your student-neighbors kept an eye on you, grabbed me when I passed down the hall, shared some worry about you, or some sweet conversation they'd had, or a plate of food they wanted you to have. There were ties, even then, of affection, learning, admiration, concern.

I guess I will miss that, too; all those vibrant folk. But I may find other ways to stay in touch, to keep my hand in the stew of what is bubbling up into the future. And I can't wait to turn the other hand toward what it loves to do – create, weave baskets, write, pick herbs.

I think you would be happy for me. I imagine I'll feel you, right there beside me, gazing over a shoulder at the newest basket, the combination of colors, how the shape is coming along, the firmness of the form. I can feel it now.

8/18/12

A short walk in the rain down to the pond where the pearly sky is pale, raindrops dimple the water, kingfishers argue over hidden fish.

And feeling a little flicker of excitement about the possibility of going somewhere south to retire – of leaving the Northeast. But what about Maine? I have loved being here so much.

How can it be that I am so many different things? Excited and scared, in love with this place, and yet, just plain done; happy to be finished with you, but still holding on. I guess I am not just one thing, not just love or joy or sweetness, exhaustion or regret or fear, but a whole, motley mess of feelings, welling up together.

I am sure you were that, too. I wonder what you are now. Do all your feelings and awarenesses finish up somehow; do they just settle into a Great Shining that showers over the world? Well...I imagine it is all of these: an easing; a letting go; a fierce grace of loving and holding on; an eagerness to share, to keep extending love.

I can see you now, face beaming, arms open so wide, still pouring out tender care over us all.

8/23/12

At the lake beach, I step into water for a swim despite an air temperature of only forty-eight degrees, mist hanging thick, and the dewy grass cold on my bare feet. Even though I will have to walk back home wet, I want to swim into the sun, slip into that light that shines over the silvery lake. So I do. Mist rolls over my face, little glimmering waves lift me up, filmy mare's-tail clouds slip over the upside-down blue bowl of the sky. Water is warmer than the air.

Bodi watches from the shore, keeps an eye on my face that rises up above the waves.

I have no thoughts – and then I do: about you, and things lost. I heard yesterday that the Upper Ridge house, my first real home here, the one I pondered buying last year but decided against, has sold. Someone will now tear it down, build a new one with windows facing the field and the dark hills.

So...finally, gone. The place that welcomed me will have to go into that box of special pleasures that can never be held again, can only shine, sweet and gentle, in a corner of my love room with life – just like you.

8/31/12

Only a few more days until your leaving day. I can feel something building – a confluence of memories, of feelings: love, sadness, joy, fear. Maybe the walls between worlds – this one, and the one you're in – are thinning as we roll toward your end-time anniversary. Surely the world that gave birth to you will turn your way, just for a moment; could never forget or fail to love what you were. Maybe there's a window. Maybe you will be leaning toward that opening, pressing your pale face close to that little portal, reaching out to touch what you loved, or just sighing fondly. I can picture that.

It feels a little easier this time. Two years gone, instead of one. Or perhaps I am just getting used to a world full of holes.

9/1/12

A dream – of family, and you. There are many people milling around, and I am trying to see a trial in a courtroom where our cousin, Mary Ann, is presiding as judge. But a security guard says I can't go in, so I sit outside and examine old family photos to see if I can recognize anyone. Then there's a big family party where everyone is dressed up. Sunny is dressed as a sheikh, wearing green plastic sandals that don't fit very well, and Dede is wearing a belly-dancing dress. Her red hair is all pulled back into hundreds of thin braids, and she smiles, and I suddenly see that she looks exactly like you. I mention that to Sunny, and he agrees. I keep gazing and gazing at her, then wake up. It was so good to see you that it's hard to let go of the dream.

I guess I am still leaning toward you and your used-to-be spot as the world swings toward your going-away time.

9/2/12

At Winslow Beach, I step into ocean water that it is pretty cold and choppy. There is sun, blue sky, a small wind, boys chasing seagulls, chatty parents. A seagull feather balances on a little crest of sand, wobbles in the breeze, lifts up and away.

You were like that: delicate, then taken by the wind.

9/3/12

Two years ago, this was your last night. You were ready. Tired of struggling, and of all the changes that were new and hard.

I sit for a while in the silence, not wanting to glance at your photo, but I do anyway, and there it is again: the truth.

Yes, you're gone. Yes, it is impossibly hard. Yes, there is still, for me, an emptiness. My eyes want to shed tears. But the nectar of your having-been is such nourishment that I am able to bear the Mystery turning itself inside out and taking you back.

Suddenly I am feeling you and your mother as if you were both inside me, inside my own body-self. Three layers of woman-lives all converging right here; a small and happy surprise. My mouth curves up in a lopsided smile.

Min early in her teaching career

Min's newly svelte figure

The quintessential Min

Year 3

Still Trying to Keep You Alive

9/7/12

Did you steal me, in some ways, capture me like you did all those men over so many years? Or like your friends, who were fiercely devoted? I'm beginning to see I volunteered for that. Part of it was the early loneliness, an innocence that needed some kind of shelter. You lifted me up onto the wings of your own life. But then later, it was easier to just slide along, pressed against you, certain that in a pinch, or when I was just plain tired of being grown up, I could call you, even if it was just to hear your voice, to talk over some problem. You would listen, and care.

Now, here I am at sixty-five, having to decide how to live on my own; how to face the world without leaning back toward you, without pressing into that comfort of knowing you're there.

Well...I guess I will. But it's so tempting to keep looking back.

9/8/12

I am so ready to amble along a new and gentler road. But what road would that be?

A little shiver of fond longing for Louisiana ripples through me: skin; tribe; family; heat; land. What is known, and still mysterious.

9/9/12

Too busy today for a long woods walk, so I head down the trail where tall wild impatiens leans, dewy goldenrod bows into the path, wetting my pant legs and Bodi's back. Bumblebees rest in the heart of pink flowers.

Questions bubble up as we walk. Is it possible for the love room to be both a blessed place and also a kind of trap? Has it grown to be more welcoming than everyday life? Why would I want to take on the world again after the close, odd comfort of grief?

I just want to lean my head against your bony little chest, hang onto you. Is that bad? Maybe not. But it is possible, I guess, for that longing to obscure the truth, its grace somehow cloaking the ordinary beauties of being here now.

9/14/12

Feeling odd, a little sad today, a little unanchored, but I don't know why.

My mom's death date is coming up, but I don't even know when it is. Why not, when yours is so engraved in my awareness?

I pore through old documents and find her death certificate. Today, her leaving day. Which makes me wonder: why do I turn so readily to you, and not to the mother of my own flesh?

9/16/12

Tonight, after a long time of quiet, the phone rings. For half a second, I think it might be you.

9/17/12

At the pond this morning, thready spirals of mist swirl toward the sun. The water's surface is dark and glassy, littered with duck feathers as mallards congregate, getting ready to fly away for warmer parts. No frogs in the shallows today, no herons – so maybe they, too, are leaving.

Leaving. Before you slip entirely away, I want to go down again to Louisiana, into that warmth, into what's left of the stories of our people. Before Sunny and the other elders do their own slipping away, I want to listen to what they remember of you and the web into which you arrived.

I don't know what I'll get by doing that, but it will be rich, maybe spicy, surely more than I have now. Maybe it will weave me into my own particular place in that tapestry of belonging.

This whole unfolding of what comes after love and loss has been so much more than I can say. Almost more than I can bear, though the bearing is an odd, joyous tenderness I wouldn't have missed for the world.

9/21/12

Why do I offer what I'm not sure I can really give? What is the connection between the intimacy of loving and the sorrow of giving everything away? How do I love without letting someone wander – or barge – into the tenderest place that should belong only to me?

Did I do that with you: turn to you before I turned to myself? Certainly in childhood. And when you were needy? Getting lost? I turned myself over, took on the heaviness of doing it all.

This morning, in the woods, we settle at the pond where many ducks crowd, leaving a silvery wake in shiny water. The great blue heron perches, motionless but alert on the log, mists swirling all around her.

Keeping an eye on me, but not flinching away. The heron knows how to stand alone, how to hoard the best of herself. But she knows, too, how to be exposed, how to stand in the early light, how to be seen and be okay. How to trust me, a little, because she has watched me come and go. But mostly she knows how to trust herself. How to wait, how to judge what's safe. And how to sail away.

9/24/12

Many dreams. In one, Grandma is suffering; she is quiet and low, sad because she knows all her children are gone. I try to explain to her that she'll be okay. I put my arm around her shoulders, hold her close.

I wonder if this is a series of truths, all piled into one dream – so many of the people that made me up: she, my dad, all the uncles and aunts, and you. I took you all in as a kind of destination, a guidepost around which to wrap the tissues of my life – now coming apart. Maybe what I need has already soaked into my cells, will continue to stir always in my heart, and I can let go. Not my best thing. But I could learn.

This morning I bump into Patsy A. We are happy to see each other, laugh and hug. How much I like her, even though we don't know each other very well. We're just neighborhood dog walkers, friendly, each of us interesting in our own way. I could get to know her better. But if I invite good people into my tender life, does that mean that you can be replaced? Would it be a betrayal to reach out? Did you permanently claim me for your own, or did I just learn so early that love meant giving everything over to someone else? I don't think you wanted that, but the circumstances of your situation in the last few years required it, for a while. Now, I have to find a new way – my own thriving forward without you.

9/25/12

A long, involved dream about your first helper, who turned out to be such a challenge. We talk about all that happened and work things out, come to forgiveness and letting go. Maybe that's a message; maybe I am headed in that direction.

I dream, too, about a woman at work. She is still grieving, even though her husband has been gone for a whole year. I tell her about you, and about my own journey – that it's been two years now, and I am still wandering that path. I explain how important it is to pay attention, and not push; to let grief unfold.

Funny that my life is lonely lately, but my dreams are chock-full of people. Except for you. I am dreaming around you, instead. I wonder why.

Today is Yom Kippur, a holy day of atonement; the doors between the worlds open for a while. Maybe the door between me and all the people I have loved, carried, wrestled with, is standing open so I can finish and get clear. Maybe I am dreaming what I can't quite do. Go back. Forgive. Let go.

At the pond this morning, a few treasures: one duck, one green heron hunting silvery fish, one muskrat sliding right over to where the heron plucks her meal out of the water. There is a little standoff – heron, muskrat, watching each other. Which would eat the other, if it could? Heron stands her ground; muskrat slips away. A lavender mist settles over the log.

9/28/12

A long day of driving to so many appointments, then visiting my friend Cathy who is sick, troubled by some potentially serious digestive problem. I am worried; I can't afford to lose anyone else!

How hard it must have been to continually lose those you loved. What courage it must have taken, to be left behind. After 102 years, you were an expert, I guess, at carrying on, loving and letting go. I had no idea.

9/29/12

Awake, still worrying about Cathy, so I go out for a walk in the rainy, dark morning, thinking about troubles. At the pond, we spot herons and ducks. Probably they have their own version of trouble. We all struggle together. The heart of life labors, shiny and tough, strong and frail.

Maybe I am growing up, am more able now to tolerate the beauty and the trials. This is life. Here we are. Here I am, and there you are, still shiny in my heart, though gone.

9/30/12

Waking early to a quiet house and nowhere to go, still thinking of Cathy and her new ill-health, her tired but spunky comment yesterday: "Well, I guess my life just couldn't be perfect." She reminds me of you. How many times, in 102 years, did something knock you flat: the loss of a friend; the shocking death of a brother or the child of an acquaintance; a war; or a terrible suffering you heard about? How often were you shocked out of whatever safe and comfortable place you'd settled into, had to revise the way you saw the world and its winding story of losses and loves?

I walk in the woods this morning to the pond, where a green heron sleeps in the rain, head tucked into a wing, peeping up for a moment to see us, then down again. A not-so-easy day for a bird. Struggles and pains gnaw at all our lives, wild and human alike. How much we all carry, each in our particular ways: the suffering of being alive, the flash of beauty, the indwelling loveliness, the raw edges that press us down. The world – the heart of all that is – wrestles and loves, labors and gives birth. Me, too, and you, for certain.

At home, a little snuggle with Bodi, who is half-napping. A phone call from Cathy, who says she feels better. A little rain that drips onto the ground and tin roof in this gray-green, quiet morning. I am loving the time, the slowness of having nowhere to go. And even the piles of things to be done: clothes slumped in stacks for the seasonal change-over; office and school stuff pending; and money work to do. Am grateful for even the chores, for the chance to catch up with my life. Rugged graces, all these things to do; blessings all around.

10/6/12

Walking over burnished, fallen leaves at the pond, where no turtles show up, but ducks squabble, mist is thick, more trees are coloring up in the woods, poison ivy leaves are scarlet, Bodi chases something wild.

A few love-room thoughts as we swing around your leaving-day anniversary and I head to Louisiana again: Can a love room disappear? How could the room of my heart ever be empty of you?

Is the world full of gauzy temples of leftover love, still-shining altars to the best of things that linger and sigh, even as time rolls forward? All these questions bubble up, each one tinged with the honey of sweet-sadness, empty-fullness, of what is both too much, and never quite enough.

Still...if it never ends, how does grief ever close its shadowy doors?

10/9/12

On waking, there is the love room, that little shell of your life, still curled up on the floor of what's left of the world.

10/10/12

I am on the way down south again, to hear more stories. I am still in search of you and family. I wonder how long it will stretch out, this curious longing that has taken hold. In any case, I am eager to be warm, to hear those voices, smell that air, walk the land.

10/11/12

Morning

In Louisiana, an early run along the levee near Hahnville, egrets flying overhead, little dirt roads curving down to the batture and the big river that is so wide and slow-moving as a shiny, lazy snake.

I sit and watch big barges and tugboats pass, see fish jump right out of the water, sniff up scents of childhood memories – if memories can smell like anything at all. I am walking with these, the feet of my now-life, over all the layers of things remembered, and wondered about, and loved.

I could make these my own: the pastures, the levee, the big river – filtered now through my own eyes, though how much of me is really you, I still don't know. Sometimes, I think I am still breathing you up in this spicy, warm, damp air – you and all your people, who are my people, too.

Afternoon

Over a lunch of boiled crabs and the best onion rings I've ever had, Nanette says there was something about you. Everyone knew when you were here, visiting; there was a kind of presence. She'd see you, walking around the place, over the land. She doesn't know yet what to call what she noticed; she'll have to think a little before she answers.

Dede comments that she wrote you many letters about what was going on in her life, but she worried so much about how the letters looked

– the spelling, the grammar – that she never mailed them. You told her, after a while, that you weren't going to write anymore because she never wrote back. Dede didn't have the heart to tell you how many letters she had written and then torn up. I wonder how much your sharpness blocked something that could have been good for both of you, especially after her mother died so young. Dede feels sad to think about those lost letters. I imagine that you would be sad, too.

Evening

At the diner where we all go for another flavorful and gigantic meal, I get to ask Sunny what he remembers about you. Not too much, he says. You were already twenty when he was born, and gone when he was growing up. Maybe you were a librarian for a while, or taught at the little school? He mostly remembers the brothers, because he hung out with them. Especially Major, who was a few years younger than you. He was "wild," Sunny says. I mention how much I liked being around him when I was young because he was so quiet. Sunny and Mary Janet laugh; that's the last thing they knew him to be. They saw him often, since he lived so close. He stayed there in the family house his whole life. They all say how sweet he was.

Then Sunny mentions the Martin-Vial feud over politics, the big break-up years. The election when Major showed up with a submachine gun at the town hall to guard the ballot box, to keep the Vials from stuffing it. Not, says Sunny, that the Martins hadn't already done that themselves. It was what folks did back then. I want to know more! But, in this tiny diner, where everyone knows everyone else, Sunny won't say much. It was such a painful time for the whole town – these two well-known and loved families, at serious odds. So sensitive, apparently, even fifty or sixty years later. Wow! What an interesting family! I wish I could ask you about it. Why did you never tell me? Maybe it was hard for you, too?

10/12/12

Morning

I am swimming in what you had, what you became, what family has turned out to be.

In case you can hear, and in case you care, I am going out this morning with Sunny and Nanette and a few friends, to the swamp where Sunny and his cronies like to fish. And though I'm tired, I think it will be good – the family wrap-around, the wilder places in the early sun. I wanted so much in my girlhood years to slip out into that hidden, watery world. I think you'd be happy to know I am going there now. I can feel you smiling.

Evening

A fun day boating. On the water, we scurried to get two boats launched, squeezed through thick brush out to the open swamp, passed giant lotus leaves cupping diamond-dew, and gallinules, ducks and yellow-billed cuckoos. Then the boat sputtered to a stop. Sunny was frustrated, wanted us to have a good time, refused to give up trying to start the motor again. But we all laughed, grabbed oars, moved slowly back to the dock, paddling through so much beauty. We took pictures of each other, called out good things to see: an errant orange tree at the bayou bank; wild hibiscus; a great blue heron; pelicans; a coyote watching us; an alligator rolling away from the boat.

10/13/12

Morning

Up early, padding over the creaky floor to peer out at the paling sky, and feeling again what could have been when I was a child, always just a little out of reach – and the glad luckiness of waking up to it now.

Today: a walk down to the river; a trip to the cemetery to see your grave marker; a family food fest; a visit with Jara; and more stories about you from Nanette.

I wonder again about yearning for this land where I grew up – the fragrant, misty closeness. Maybe it's like the food here; once you've tasted what flavor and spice can be, nothing else is enough.

Where will my future rest, I wonder: Maine? Or Louisiana? Could my feet walk on two different places and call them both home? I don't know. For now, crows call from tall trees, sky glows misty orange, boat horns hoot up from the river.

10/14/12

I walk down to the batture beach, where the river is churning and brown. A fish flips up and out of the water, plunges back in, over and over – silver in the hot sun.

And trash, all along this little strip of sand; dumped from busy tug boats or scooped up by some stormy wind and tossed ashore. The water worries me. Is the fish that flips out of the water jumping away from chemicals that burn its tender flesh? Is it hungry for air? The sand isn't much better: bits of plastic; broken soda bottles; a hospital mask; and old tubes of industrial lubricant.

I gather up whatever I'm not afraid to touch, stack it into piles to pick up later and haul away. While I work, killdeer slip along the curve of damp sand.

Back at Nanette's, everyone gets ready for tonight's meal, talks about the football game and which team will win. Jara calls to say the toad lilies are in bloom – can we come for tea?

I wonder what led you to leave this closeness; this gentle, attentive life; the gorgeous food and fun and family ties – and even feuds; the long chats with anyone who dropped by?

Did your Maryland life in that little cave of a condo seem pretty sparse sometimes? Or were you happy to get away from what could, I guess, seem a bit much? Either way, you missed it enough to keep coming back for more

And will I keep coming back for more; decide to sink new roots into this familiar, fertile ground? I don't know. For now, there are ribs smoking, muffins baking, cousins waiting with tea, sun heating things up, bags of trash picked up from the river beach to lug away, more stories to hear.

Afternoon

A little trip to the cemetery to find your coming-in and going-out dates finally inscribed: 1908 to 2010. You get credit for all your years. I sit for a while on the cement top of your tomb. I try to say something to you, but there are, oddly, no words. I don't want to stay. But I don't want to turn around and walk away, either.

I wish it were beautiful here. I wish this small, whitewashed cemetery wasn't surrounded by the pumping, swishing, belching smokestacks of the chemical plant. I wish it was quiet. At least, then, I could walk away knowing you're somewhere lovely. But there's just the surreal starkness of death – yours, Helen's, Johnny's, Major's, Grandma and Papa's – the many relatives. There is just the unreality of you in that tiny box, surrounded by the lush emerald land fanning out all around.

Maybe tomorrow I'll bring flowers. I'm pretty sure you don't need anything from me, but the brightness of a few petals can't hurt.

10/15/12

Morning

Another walk across the levee to the river beach where, even though I stuffed one garbage bag with trash yesterday, the sand is littered again:

red plastic hardhat; hospital masks; the many empty soda bottles and caps; brushes; bits of colored plates; and a few sodden curves of tree bark.

I pile a few things to bag up and feel sad. So much is slipping away. I want to hold onto it all: this land, green and velvety, flat and wide; the river my dad knew; the fragrant air; a kitchen bubbling with what feeds more than my belly, the door always open – and family, and you.

Late Afternoon

Nanette and I sit in the shadowy kitchen and talk. She shares a memory of you, wearing a gray dress, walking around the yard alone, deep in your own thoughts.

When you came to Hahnville, she says, everyone knew you were here. You had gone away, studied, traveled the world; so rare for someone from this tiny town. But you were both theirs and also, only, your own. Even though she could walk with you, she says, there was always a kind of aloofness, a distance, an enclosure another person couldn't enter.

That makes me a little sad, like Dede's comment about all the letters she didn't send. Both of them loved you, but felt kept out. I wonder if you noticed. I felt it, too, for so long. Was it a way to keep some place for yourself in that wild, motley press of relations?

Nanette talks about family, says someone commented once that the Vials were a tribe – whole unto themselves. A person could enter in from the outside, be welcomed and loved, but the family didn't go outside the circle much for companionship. That is true of her, Nanette remarks. When she wants to do something fun or interesting, with someone she likes, she thinks of Dede or Monica or Lauren.

And there is the link with land, the "root," she calls it – where seven generations have walked and lived and made a home. A pretty amazing thing, especially these days.

Evening

On the plane north, I wonder what I am left with that is more than an interesting tangle of kin, your small box of ashes in the weird graveyard, and the terrible tenderness that never seems to end.

On this small, fragile plane, going home, I am hoping that my own life, my small snatch of time, is held aloft, loved fiercely, lived well.

10/16/12 in Portland

How much more about you can I know, now that all the tales, and the people who could tell them, are fading away? I am trying to fill the hole you left. Getting to know the Hahnville people helps some, but it's really an impossible thing, for who is replaceable, after all? Not one of us. Not one stone or flower or pet. Not one cloud.

10/18/12

I talk with Nanette on the phone. She couldn't leave home today because the tree men were coming to trim away dead wood, cut rickety limbs off the live oaks that are one hundred or two hundred years old. She couldn't bear to be away, to not stand guard. Even her dog was watchful.

So that is how we are: inextricably tied to a place where we've sunken deep roots – which is certainly true for me.

10/20/12

In the light, misty rain this morning, the air smells like Hahnville. The dampness, the summer-lush leaves turning toward fall, brings a little twinge of that place, and of you.

But the fact is: you're gone. What I have left of you now are my own skin and tissues and bones, the walls of my heart, the family I am getting to know, the persistent longing I've tried to keep at bay. Maybe I can stand you being gone, even though the thought gives me chills. How short our lives really are. One hundred years is just a flash on the surface of time, bounded on all sides by what is immutable – the end. Our end. But we manage not to know, not to think ahead, to focus our sight, instead, on going toward what still could be.

Now, I have to move on without you, which just rips my own going forward into shreds.

10/26/12

I am telling stories about you lately, about my aunt who died at 102 and what she used to say. It still feels wrong. I am pasting a small patch over a gigantic hole and expecting that to work; pretending that I can move on, that you're a good, rich tale instead of that large emptiness just out of sight.

11/4/12

Hahnville pulls at me, like sun on a flower whose petals want to open in just this particular way, whose face wants to turn in just that direction. Surely that must mean something?

Do I still want to turn back to you, and those people who hold up the stuff out of which we were made? Could I do both for a while: turn toward what you and I came from, and also lay down the road of my own going forward? For how can I weave a future without using the threads of the past? My going forward will be a tapestry of the riches and loves, missed chances and mysteries, of all that came before, knotted into my own love room with life. Our love room will keep throbbing, breathing, sighing, in whatever I do.

And what will you be in that tapestry? A shimmery bundle of silken threads, a few gnarly knots, a strong warp in the woven fabric of my life? I am sure that's true.

Can I lay you down, then, if I know that you will always flicker up in whatever joyful thing I do, whatever hard thing I undertake, whatever my future could become?

11/9/12

This morning the sky is just lightening when we walk, trees black in the indigo dawn, wind feisty. My body is cranky with pain, mind chock-full of busy work thoughts. At the pond, ducks sail over the shiny quicksilver water; a muskrat splashes; two squawking great blue herons circle overhead, just above the pines.

At home, I sit in the bedroom rocker as sun slips into the window. I pull your shawl up into its place over the back of the rocking chair, say hello, and smile. Are you there? I hope so. Lately these little wisps of you are all I've got.

11/11/12

After a busy day of too many things to do, I light the little candle in the bedroom and think of you. I miss out time together, miss pulling away from the crushing, distracted busyness of life. I want the little cave of sinking down, of being still, of the lush quiet place where we can meet up. That seems so hard to come by these days.

11/13/12

Oh, my heart wants to stretch out into so many directions: to follow the fading footprints of your life; to sit in a little corner with our people so we can touch one another, talk and smile about you, and remember; plot whatever future there will be without you.

11/16/12

How can so much of the love my heart poured out in your direction be going nowhere now? Does it just spill into the universe, grow thin and pale, disappear? Or does it somehow collect, settle into a special pocket of wonderful things, help to hold up the great going-forward of the world?

I have to think that this is true.

11/17/12

Your stuff is staring me in the face. I am impatient. How many unopened boxes still claim bits of my time, of my future? How many things are there still to go through?

Enough! I want my life back! I want to plow through all those crates, filled with trinkets saved, letters from decades ago. I want to look at what I couldn't for so long, and chuck much of it out –though I feel irreverent thinking that. I want to pass through my dining room without seeing the litter of things I haven't had time, or heart, to take on.

I still love you. I am sure there are treasures tucked into places where I tossed them in the pressured flurry of emptying your house. But I want to get through. I need to pull together the scattered, long-ignored shards of my own life and time, and be here, now. This time is mine.

Will I miss you forever? Will I keep turning back to you? Maybe not so much.

11/19/12

After much busyness, this is my first morning to just be slow, to sit at the pond that is stitched into a silvery sheet of ice glinting in the early sun. The muskrat is rolling, just beneath the surface of the water, sailing back and forth from her den.

Today, no frenzied, helter-skelter thoughts, but a few gentler ones. Reflections on Peter, with whom I am spending more time. You'd love his energetic, quirky-minded self! And of Mike, and what seems to have settled into just a friendship, and whether that's okay.

And Hahnville. Am I still trying to find some new place to belong, now that the place you held for me is disappearing? Am I still looking for a new home ground? How would that work? Maybe it's just something I have to try.

I wish I could ask what you'd think of the idea. You might be curious, cautious, excited – which are, of course, all the things I am feeling, too. Maybe a part of you is still living just beneath my skin, looking forward with my eyes, leaning toward that place my heart seems to want. I can imagine that.

11/22/12

Thanksgiving Day. A good thing, to give thanks. I take the turkey out of the bag, wash and oil the heavy, drooping body, shimmy it into the pan and then the oven, remember past Thanksgivings and people loved. The best part of most celebrations: sharing the joy and the troubles; all the work; and then time for play.

Still, I want to resist, want to choose the thick grayness of loss, as if being happy would be "the end." If I were happy, I would have to face the realness of you being gone. If I did things with people, the yawning, empty truth would flood right in. If I tore through the caul of your death, I would break into unbearable freedom. If I stop writing, you will disappear.

I am still waiting at the door of what will never return.

Are you worried about me, and how reluctant I seem to be to move on? I am, too, a little. What would you say about this pall? Maybe a sad, worried ripple would pass across your face. And then a bracing up, shoulders squared, a graceful bark, a reminder to pull up out of those woeful thoughts, shape up, do what needs to be done. Self-pity only complicates things, you'd say. And with a quip, a twinkle in your eye, you'd give me a hard hug.

But I think you'd understand, for, even though you forged on after Papa died, and Grandma, Johnny, my dad, Fred, Helen, and Tine—I know you thought about them. I know some part of you looked back to where they still might be. I think you'd agree that something lingers—a breathy place where souls can touch, lean against each other, even after the end.

Well... this morning brings a little visit with Peter; he is already excited that I'll come. Then the gathering with friends afterwards, which will be good. But I'll miss talking with you. My ear still longs to hear your voice. Blessings, Sweet One; many thanks for you.

12/1/12

Is life just a downward spiral of loss, a long journey of giving things up? Were you the shifted boulder that loosened the tumbling flood of so many other things being washed away? What can I count on, if everything can be gone? What am I, if not planted in a context of connections?

Maybe all these losses are meant to drive us inward, to whatever lasts – into Mystery, the ineffable sweetness of being.

Air is gray this morning with the tiniest snowflakes. I hope it thickens and piles up. In this cold, the trees, the plants, could use some cover, and I need more than brown, more than the carpet of crisped, fallen leaves, those leftovers of what was alive.

12/2/12

So much of me is shifting since you're gone. All of my life I have leaned into what was around me, trying to find my place, the right way to be: a person; a group to take cues from; a parent I can learn how to please; a partner I can follow, or fight against. And you, who taught me it is possible to be in this world, to be your own quirky and dignified self. This is something I still need to learn, now without you.

It's a wrenching undoing of attachments, of any safe shadow in which to walk.

12/3/12

A slow-going, early walk along icy ledges in the woods and down to the pond. Only the spit of sleety rain pecking at my jacket makes any sound. Even the muskrat channel in the thick skin of ice is still – no sign of movement.

We sit for a short while, watching ice, the gray sky, the bare-boned trees. If you could watch silence, this would be it: the iced-in pond on a gray winter day.

Then home, where Bodi sleeps in a curl on the living room couch, the window lets in paltry light from the shades-of-gray day. And I read an email from Wayne Vial, a second cousin I've never met and who lives in South Carolina. He sent an obituary of a relative who has died, one of the last of your generation, though not quite as old as you were. Wayne wants us to gather as much information about the family as we can so our children can know their roots. It makes me want to go down to meet him, to share what I have of you – photos, letters, documents.

Have I become a hostage to my "tribe," gotten swept up into this swelling tide of ancestors; all the tales passed down; all the Southern land where we grew a whole big family; a rich, fertile, and dark swamp where I could sink down if I'm not careful?

But, isn't that what I wanted?

12/4/12

Another Christmas coming – two of them, now, that you've been gone.

You should see Peter. He's so tall. He loves noisy, fast, busy, scary things, fierce things. He loves worms. And pretending, though he knows that real is better than pretend. He loves sitting in the back of his dad's truck, and eating at McDonald's, and being at home with his mom and dad after they've worked all week. He's an at-home guy.

And he likes numbers; we play counting games when I'm driving. "How many noses are in this car?" I ask. He yells out, "Three!" because Bodi is with us, and dog noses count, too.

Are you seeing all this, watching us weave our lives together as we play and wrestle with things? I don't know how this works – you, being gone, maybe checking in on all of us. But wherever hearts have touched, maybe loving ears still listen. I'm pretty sure you're still leaning our way.

12/5/12

Lately, despite all the busyness of finishing up the semester and getting ready for the holiday crunch, I seem to be lightening up. I can get things done. The house is not a complete shambles. I'm not too far behind.

Could it be you, easing away? Or me, starting to recover?

12/16/12

Cold today, at sixteen degrees and windy. Overhead, a few brown leaves tick against each other like withered but still hopeful, clapping hands, remembering what there was to love, to celebrate.

Are you still loving the world; loving this place where you touched down for what seems now like such a short time? Are you showering us all with spangled smiles and sighs of fondness? Do you see how much we worry about the silliest things – power, position, getting ahead – while we are blind to what is right in front of us – wonders, and beloveds at risk: children; the earth; and all things innocent?

Are you part of the Great Tender Heart that poured us all out and still longs for her children to know joy? To see the graces? To drink them up? To give birth to peace?

I imagine that is so – that you still long for the best for all of us. In that, you are not alone.

12/17/12

A beautiful snow falling: sparkly and rose-tinted in the ambient city light.

Tonight, Christmas cards: scribbling notes, flipping through address book pages, scratching out the names of those who've drifted away. I come to your name. My finger moves to the page, brushes across your listing as if – what? – I could touch you? Brush your little hand, tucked somehow into those few words?

I can't cross out your name; instead, rub a finger over it again. You are still in there, in those old, stained, and dog-eared pages, your whole life pressed into a few dark, squiggly lines.

It was nice, to find you there.

Now, Bodi hops onto the bed, a candle flickers, snow is thick in the sky outside the window.

12/24/12

Yesterday, in the midst of Christmas busyness and finishing up school work, I volunteered to help Lara move: meet her at her old apartment; load up our cars; schlep stuff over to the new place. But she was late, and there were a few "found" moments to just sit still, so I did. Sat there in my car on that cold city street, watching.

Nearby, two women got out of a car, walked toward the building. The wind buffeted their coats. They were well-dressed, talking, smiling. Both had white hair. The taller woman leaned forward, held her companion's arm, wrapped herself around the shorter, older woman to shield her from the gusts. Her hair was cut in a stylish bob that flipped into her face, but I could see her smile, their smiles. Feel the love between them. They were so happy to be with each other. They were beautiful. I almost pulled out my camera to take a picture of them, but they slipped inside the building and were gone.

They reminded me of you, of us, of how sweet and good it felt, all those years, to wrap myself around you, to hold on so you wouldn't slip – oh, that happy privilege.

The women came out again, moved toward their car. The taller woman glanced up at me. Amazing how much she looked like you – her narrow nose, the sparkle in her smile. Our eyes met. We both knew, in that flash of a glance, how lucky they were, to have and enjoy each other. Like we were lucky, too.

Love is contagious, and enough. These strangers, hanging onto one another, remind me.

12/25/12

Christmas evening

After a bustling, busy, exhausting, and mostly fun day, I sit in the quiet house, alone. Outside, snow is beautiful on this dark, cold night. The moon shines, nearly full. A planet hangs very close by, as if it is leaning into that light.

Tonight, in a longing to restore some normalcy after such a harried, busy time, I am digging through one of your boxes. I have been through it already, months ago, but ended up stuffing everything back in. What to do with all the old pictures that are not quite good enough, or unnamed, and that probably no one wants, yet are still precious since they belonged to you? I am tired of them all, impatient with being the keeper of the remnants of your life. I don't want to keep living in the boxes of the past – not even yours. I throw out a stack of blurry, yellowed photos; a start.

12/26/12

Sick, with stuffy head, coughing, sneezing, cloudy thinking, so not much got done today. Still, things keep happening around me: an oil delivery I have to spend my vacation money to afford; more new snow to shovel in the dark; a visit from Lara, who insists she wants to help, so brings a space heater, a door-stopper to keep out cold drafts. She asks for more to do. I give her the chore I've been putting off: giving up on the huge Hoya plant that hung in that sunny kitchen window before I moved here but never thrived in the sparse city light. So many lovely memories tied to it; I hesitate to give them up when, lately, loveliness is so hard to come by.

Lara takes it out into the deep, still-falling snow, despite her fancy holiday shoes. She talks to the plant, thanking it for its life, comes back happy to have gotten rid of it and, more, to have done something for me.

Letting go; not one of my talents, so far.

12/30/12

I cancel my vacation because I am too sick to go, although the idea of trying to make it through a Maine winter without heat and sun is a struggle. Sad, too, not to be able to see Louisiana folks. I am missing family; I think you would understand.

Now, Bodi tucks into a towel on the bed, licks snow from his paws after a walk. Windows are frosted with melting ice, sky is a little lighter, me a little sad and bereft over losing my time with Vials – and Mexico, of course. I am also a little relieved at having more time just to be slow. A hard grace, I guess.

1/1/13

New Year's Day

How much we have to let go of in this life. How necessary it is to ease up on the way we think things should be because, really, they never are. Life makes itself up from the threads of so many ways and needs, choices and unexpected turns. And what can you do, then, but wrap your heart around what really happens; let your gaze, the eyes of love, follow what gives birth to itself; learn something new about the graces of a complicated heart?

Oh, the things you can't predict. In your 102 years, you certainly knew that. For all your attention and careful work, planning and wisdom and willingness to forego today against a long line of tomorrows, you still couldn't control everything – in fact, not much, as it turned out.

Your heart had to make way for shocks and twisty turns, betrayals and follies and happy surprises. Those graces you hadn't expected – how to be vulnerable and tender, how to cry with joy, how to be soft – all slipped in without you noticing.

I guess my heart will follow yours down that humble, winding road. I will be surprised, too. I already am.

1/5/13

Finally on my way to Louisiana, a softness steals over me. I don't know why I need to go back, but something's gotten into me that keeps tugging, so here I am, following along.

Evening

Tonight Nanette cooks gumbo. We chat in the kitchen about family – who is fine and who is troubled – a good and gentle time.

Later, going to bed, I realize that, ninety-eight years ago today, two houses down from here, my dad was born at home, youngest of the clutch of six. You probably waited for him – one more brother to scoop up and love.

1/6/13

Layers of story and kinship. Like Nanette says about cooking, and flavors, and all the work of putting food together, it's the timing and care that count – one stage done, then the next, with nothing ignored. Every step is all love and attention, details and patience, savoring.

So family is, too, I guess. Here I am, wrapped in these layers of place and memory and kin. And, oh, the warmth; oh, the land that still feels like my body – so well-known. Oh, the people – those who are gone, those who carry forward. We talk about somehow creating an archive of the families –Vials and Martins – a place to house keepsakes. Maybe

I could put some of your things there, photos that might otherwise get tucked into a distant relative's old albums, all the stories forgotten. A tangible, living love room, here at the root of the root; that could be good.

Now, sodden ground outside the window shines with silvered puddles in gray light.

1/8/13

Last night, just as color drained from the sky, I walked out the back door and over the tough grass toward what used to be Keet's – the little orchid house, the expanse of field between her place and Grandma's. I tried to see with the eye of my heart what isn't there anymore, walk those spaces with my grownup body that remembers how it measured out for little-girl legs.

Do all these realities cancel each other out? How could it be that my body remembers so well, with so much longing, what isn't true anymore? This place, it turns out, is a complicated thatch of memory and truth, tinted all the colors of love.

1/9/13

Here I am, at this earliest root of "home," where loving and history and belonging wrapped around me from all directions and I was left alone in the best of ways – given space, and time, to be curious, explore the old house, run acres of field past all the wild growth, my fledgling thoughts rising up and blooming any old way they could. That richest world, made safe with the rounded corners of attention and sweet faith that we, the kidlings of the family, would find our way home when we were ready.

And so I have. There's something about losing you that has made me scramble back to the place where we both hatched. To reach out, touch familiar things we shared, even if it was at far-distant times. I have to believe something must be real and permanent. So, here I am.

1/10/13

Getting ready to go, I want to soak up so many things – scents, green tangles of brush, bird songs, arched arms of the live oak trees.

No visit to your grave so far this trip. Will you miss me, with whatever thin slip of you might still linger? Will part of you always wait there for me? I think you'd be too practical for that. But here I am, trying to stuff my heart with all these good things before I go.

Now, wind picks up, oak branches sway. No great rain so far, but it will come, they say: one-hundred-percent chance. And me? There's a one-hundred-percent chance I'll be coming back.

1/11/13

In Portland, I walk this morning over packed snow in the twenty-four-degrees air, into the woods where sun steals over the pond, over the pebbled ice. I sit on a snowy bank to catch the light and small warmth, let thoughts bubble up and spread out, and gentle questions hang in the air – about choices, needs, and what I want: a quiet life, taking care of my health, rest, and play.

Once again, both in Louisiana and here, it is land that anchors me: a place my body remembers, the way my bones settle into the slumps and hillocks of what's known; the skin of my life, knitted from the things I've loved.

I am guessing this is true for everyone. I have heard that newborn infants are biologically programmed to bond with what is around them during their first twenty-four hours: a mother, a family, if that's available; an incubator, if not. I am guessing this interweaving of our lives doesn't stop there, at that birth moment. Surely we continue to knit the skin of our lives from the fabric of what's around us, always. And so I have.

1/13/13

Despite worries about how to take care of money, how to stay afloat on this uncharted sea of aging, there is the little loveliness of being able to choose what I want – a new, rare gift.

Even the idea that I am going to be alone doesn't feel so bad now. Did you love that? Did you sink into the small cave of your life as if it were a warm fire, a nourishing meal, made just for you?

I wish I could ask you these things. I wish I had pulled up out of my petty concerns, the daily management chores, and asked you more. You might have been glad to share the journey of your life, the trail of decisions. Are they still here, around me, in the tracks of your choices? Maybe I will find them in your letters, still unopened.

Now, Bodi sleeps in a mess of blankets tangled on the bed. The room is chilly, my belly warm with hot tea. Sky is gray outside the window. Heat is creaking through the vents.

1/19/13

Alison texts about what Peter and I will do today. I check the internet for what's happening at the Children's Museum, and think how much you would have loved this – such easy access to the gigantic pool of information available these days, without dictionaries, encyclopedias and research. Though maybe you would have still loved books – their small heft, the leisurely chance to pluck out whatever caught your eye. I love that, too.

And there it is again: that tender, painful tugging at the wound of you being gone.

1/25/13

Today I cleaned up my bedroom altar, where your picture stands alongside other things I love: a box of desert stones, an osprey feather, Daddy's old plastic statue of the Virgin Mary with half a broken halo, the little wooden carving of the Profound Buddha who can absorb the sorrows of the world, a picture of a polar bear who looks like she is praying, Lara's collage from last Mother's Day. I dusted the surface, threw out a few things, put your photo back in its spot, cleaned out the candle holder, lit a new flame.

I know you're gone. I know you're not coming back – that you must get to go completely at some point. But it's too hard, the knowing. How can this be? I still feel you, in the tiniest pressure against my skin, a breathy sigh in the air all around, something shifting in my brain. Am I okay, without you? Will all this be fine, somehow? I don't know what to think.

1/27/13

A walk in the eight-degree-cold morning to the pond, where crow calls rattle up from dark woods, sun steals over bare trees to spill, golden, over the tired, knobbly ice. Then hurrying home to sit in the rocker, make notes while sun seeps through gray clouds and Bodi settles into sleep. My pen scritches over the page; me, keeping track of myself.

How many times did you do this? How many snippets of a day were stolen so you could write down all the fluttery scraps of your days to see where you stood? Could lay out questions and sink deep, watch for answers, learn something new about yourself, or the world?

I found them, you know – notebooks you grabbed up, scribbled in, kept for yourself. I threw some away before I realized what they were: you, parsing out the patterns of your life. It must have been a good thing, that necessary time: a small campfire to sit around so you could watch the flicker of your life and feed the flames.

Maybe soon there'll be time for me to look through more of your old journals. I think it will help me to see where you've been. Maybe I'll learn something about you and our people, and myself.

Now – Bodi snores from the rumpled bed he's made of my robe. Sun finally reaches over the crest of trees and warms my face. The first of prism rainbows show up on the wall. Maybe I've sat, and written, long enough to keep up the fire, the love room, of my own life. I don't know if this writing gives anything to you. I don't know if this place – the airy room of our interwoven lives – needs tending anymore. But I am still loving it, still checking in once in a while to see what's there. It might be you.

1/28/13

A rosy dawn. A dream with so many parts: You are in a nursing facility and I am doing work for you. You've been sharp and bright and talkative, still seem to be healthy. Then the nurses tell me that you have stabbed seven of the workers. You seemed fine, then your black eyes glittered and you slashed at them. I feel relieved that people know this about you, because then you can stay in the hospital, and I won't have to keep figuring out what to do.

What does this mean? Am I trying to get rid of you, and be done – or did you do this to me? Kill me off in a small way no one could see? Well, my health did fall apart when I was trying to live both our lives. And here I am now, trying to recover.

I feel guilty about dreaming this, even though we can't control our dreams. Maybe I'm sorting out all the conflicting emotions and realities around having helped, and been so mad at, and loved so fiercely, and then lost, you.

1/30/13

Wanting, lately, in this exhausted state of my health, to do quiet things: to just sink into all the letters I've written to you over these past couple of years, trace the long line of bruises; those tender, painful joys. They might make a bridge over what is broken. Which would be my heart.

2/5/13

A dream of Sunny's story about how little they had during the war. Everyone wanted him to play basketball because he was tall, but the only clothes they could afford were women's pants that dyed his legs blue when he sweated, and sneakers so short his toenails curled over after a while and finally fell off.

My dreams keep going back to what was known and loved. It seems so natural that beloved times and folks have woven themselves into my skin. That part of my body-mind keeps turning in those directions. But I wonder how these things I've collected might be weighing me down.

Do we all do this? Gather up the beloved dust of what's already gone that then becomes the lens through which we see the world? Is nothing then seen clearly? Do we love the lens through which we look so much we forget that birthing requires a space, a juicy emptiness in which something new can sprout up, come to life? At this age – almost sixty-six – how much of what I lean toward will be new? The past has had its day. Beloveds linger in the heart. But I'm still alive, even if you're not. And I want the road forward to be free. I want to be surprised, to stumble into something new. I hope I have the courage to let that come true.

2/10/13

My friend Susan's mother died, finally, on Friday, after years of being increasingly limited and difficult to live with. Susan says her mom's last hours were not peaceful; instead, they were noisy, fraught with frenzied doctors and nurses coming and going as her mother dwindled. Her mother, Susan says, knew she was dying, though no one would listen. Susan would have liked to sit with her mom, hold her hand, forgive, love, pray. Instead she was jostled and worried, pressed to make decisions, and then kept away at the end.

What a grace, that you were able to do it your own way: sitting in the chair, watching out the window, caught up in quiet prayer, sighing into Mystery all by yourself.

How like you. Now, even though I didn't get to be there, I am glad for you. It sounds like a better way to go.

2/13/13

Some drifty thoughts this morning as Bodi snuggles close, about retirement, money, the future. You gave me the possibility of something besides being frantic with need as I age. My life will be sustained. I can step away from the hot, edgy breath of busyness, and claim a little rest.

How did I end up at the top of your list of people to love? You have built me a bridge. I wonder why.

2/15/13

At the airport at 4 a.m., I wolf down a sausage and cheese omelet and then step onto the plane to Mexico. It still feels so odd, to be going somewhere other than toward you, or at least toward our family. In a few days it will be your 105th birthday. How could I even know someone who was 100, 102? How could I reach back a whole century?

I am the throbbing extension of a whole line of people. I miss them – and you.

Finally we are up and off. Outside the plane window, the silvery metallic wing shines in the sun. Down below, filmy, breathy clouds move, and beneath them, the ground – a gray-white palette of ice, snow, places now indistinct from so far away. And you – indistinct? Not in my heart's eye.

2/17/13

Morning

Tomorrow is your birthday. I'll bet the universe still celebrates. Ethereal bells still chime for you, for every loved one born, even after they're gone.

You're still my aunt, even if you're not "you" anymore. Maybe you've been absorbed into the drifty stuff of the universe, the stars overhead, the air we breathe, or dreams. There's still your day, tomorrow – your little portal into time. I wonder if you remember. Do you still blush with the joy of it all, your small throb of a life?

Lara is down in Louisiana visiting Celeste. I asked them to bring you flowers. I think you'd like to know that there's a little gathering of our folk. I imagine Lara helping Celeste with her ragged garden, the two of them probably laughing, maybe squabbling, and surely loving. I'm glad they have each other. I'm glad we all had you. My eyes want to cry, even though something in me has been able to let go a bit. My mind understands, but my body? Probably never.

How could we look at the possibility of our own disappearing, and not be stunned into disbelief?

I've been thinking of my mom lately. I'm a little sad that I withheld love. Now, I wish I could ask her what she thought about things.

Especially as I age, and you're not here, I wonder about her. Maybe I'm building another bridge backward – a little healing of what wasn't, that could have been. All these things are in my head, my heart, on the eve of your birthday.

Afternoon

I sit outside for tea and a visit from the neighborhood iguana. "Grampa Iggy," I have named him, with his wild, orange-and-pink, bumpy skin, wide black bands along his tail. He is grizzly and stupendous. Snaps up bits of juicy grapefruit I toss onto the cobbled stones where he waits and watches me. They sleep under the porch, he and his smaller mate who is gray-green and less assertive. Scaly bodies rustle over fallen palm branches as they slip into the shadowy dark beneath the floor. I hear them moving around under my chair. After being here in Cozumel only a few days, it seems perfectly natural now to see them sitting in the sun, to hear them shifting under the porch – Iggy, who likes grapefruit and keeps his three eyes on me, and his shy wife.

Well...there is not much else to say, but I don't want to stop writing. Then you'd be gone. Maybe I'll see you in my dreams.

2/18/13

Oh, it's your birthday again! I am here. You might be, too, but I can't know. I wish I were with Celeste and Lara in Louisiana; then there'd be three of us together who knew and loved and wrestled with you. We might be making a soft spot where you could land your airy self, if you were so inclined. That would be sweet.

I guess you are landing, anyway, in our hearts. That soft tether is still intact.

2/20/13

Love is a chain. If I love friends, I can never leave them. If home is the Upper Ridge house, I can't move far away. If I love my daughters, I will do what they want. If I love you, I will hunker down at the door of the love room forever, lonely and lost.

But what of the life that bubbles up in me, just wants to go its own particular way? Follow its own course, overflow its banks, maybe make a new stream? What about that? Though my heart still stretches back to friends, places, you, I am still – always – new. My future, stretching out ahead, will remember you. But it will be looking forward. That has to be true.

Today I am off to see Mexican ruins, snorkel and ride around the island. I believe that you'll be there, somehow, too, in these places you touched so many years ago. Maybe all of us who have ever been and then gone leave a small bit of the skin of our souls wherever we've trod. So you're both gone, and here: two different truths. So many truths, all swelling up and around each other in this stream of a life.

2/23/13

We all have our little ways: the particular order of how we go about a thing, what feels just right. Back in our Portland house, Bodi slumps into the room, hops onto the bed, tosses his curly head, paws the covers into a little nest. He mumbles to himself, flops down in my spot, even though he knows I will nudge him over when I'm ready to sleep. It's just what he does. You and I had our habits, too – how we'd sit across from each other in your quiet living room; I'd work on a basket, you'd read and pray and rest your eyes. All those tiny pearls at the edges of the sturdy fabric of a life.

2/24/13

Feeling exhausted, and wondering about retirement and where to go. I need a warmer place, but I love Maine so much. How can I leave a place where all my jumbly parts slide together into a whole? Where, everywhere I turn, there is beauty? Where the trees speak to me, the waters whisper as they hold me up? Where, underneath the busied habit of a life, there is this: the small, satisfied smile of living smack in the midst of wonders?

In Louisiana, there could be warmth and lushness and our tribe. But how could I live in a place where I can't see stars, or swim in fresh water? What will anchor me? And who?

Now, lacy, irregular flakes of snow pour out of the gray sky, pile up in the yard, frost fenceposts and tree limbs. Even without you, there is always something to love.

2/26/13

After a walk in squishy and refrozen snow, Bodi sleeps in his nest of blankets, scents of doggie spit and pine sap rising up – familiar and comforting. His raggedy head, his lifting eyebrows as he watches to see what I'm doing. I am his familiar. Home. We all need that – a well-known direction to lean into. Even though he loves going somewhere else for a while, like Eleanor's camp – romping through woods, tearing over fields after the wild turkeys – he still wants to come back, race to his well-known spots: the couch, the bed where he buries his head in pillows. Love might be leaning toward what we know. And where we're known.

It is hard to lean toward you now, but my body is getting used to your airiness, I guess. I am learning something about love, loss, what to lean toward, how to let go, how to "seize the day." Sometimes, that's all we have. And, oh, what a grace.

2/27/13

Tomorrow is my birthday! We still have birthdays together in this stretch of the shortest month. Surely the mother-world must still celebrate that opening, out of which any of us are born.

As usual on my birthday, I am wondering if you'll slip in to say hello, though I believe you are probably pretty anchored wherever you are. Somewhere away from me.

2/28/13

I'm beginning to understand a little bit of the tender joy you had over the smallest things – a birthday card, a fine bit of chocolate, a ripe strawberry. I guess everything becomes something to savor after a while.

This morning, walking in inches and inches of wet, sloppy, mushy snow, and then rushing to get to work, there is still joy. A neighbor brings over his snowmobile as I am trying to clear the driveway for my car, and takes down the snow boulders in a few noisy sweeps. And I get a happy hello from neighbors, a birthday card stuck in my apartment door. Life loves us in so many small ways.

You knew that.

3/8/13

Everything around us this morning is white, white. Strong winds lift puffy sheets of snow up out of trees whose bare branches clack together.

On the woods path, two trees stand twined around each other, snow falling only so far into their embrace. I don't know why they catch my eye. Things grow together after a while, I guess. No matter how tall and straight you are, there is the tendency to lean, to press close. So this oak has grown smack into that tall pine, stretched two hefty branches right into its heart. Do the trees remember, I wonder, what it was like to be alone, to be just one, to feel the wind, the sun on all surfaces of their long, dark skins?

And what was that first impulse to move in close, to tilt toward presence instead of air? Did one of them hold back, the other tease and then take the first step? Was it a curious thrill, that first pressing of smooth bark to rough, of needles to leaves? Did it just become habit, then, that mingling, until they forgot what it was to stand alone? Until they were this: the marriage trees, facing weather and time as if they were one?

And what will happen if one of them falls? That's what I want to know. For here I am, still waking up every day in a world without you.

3/9/13

Happy plans to visit my friend Sarah in North Carolina, then meet up with Wayne Vial. He is willing to drive from his home in South Carolina so we can get to know one another, compare photos and old keepsakes. A new road back to the richness of family, of you.

It will be warm; the southern air, the sun, and family and friends. I wonder what I'll find out from Wayne that I don't already know. An amazing thing you have become, even in your absence; a little untangling of the mystery of who we were. I think you'd like that.

I wonder if that will add another fresh rivulet to the ocean of our lives. I am happy to be finding out.

3/11/13

Sitting near the window, I reach up to stretch, hook my arms over the back of the chair. My hands press flat against your shawl. Oh! Even without knowing it, my body still reaches toward you.

3/21/13

I believe you've gone on. I know I have to let you go. Still, it is the most natural thing in the world for me to want to tell you things.

At school, though I have been so good at staying disengaged from struggles, I end up smack in the middle, trying to help. I guess that's what happened with you – I cared, so I ended up holding the center, carrying the load. In this case, I will try to stay neutral, speak my piece, slip back into the shadows – but it's a tricky thing, given my bent toward solving things. A wobbly kind of balance, at best.

On the lighter side – a little talk yesterday with Nanette, who is out at Lake Martin with her cousin Claire, taking pictures of wildlife. She asks when I am coming down, and I want to say, "Now!" But it will be May before I can go. She says she'll take me to the lake to see all the wild things. That would be so good.

And Jara writes to say that it is seventy-eight degrees there, and beautiful, the air sweet with lemon blossoms and those banana shrub flowers. Remember them, that strangest sweet smell in the world?

What a warm thing all these connections are. Even though I don't have you, I have that to go back to – land, and blood. I want to share all the excitement with you; we could talk about who's related to whom, and how. But it's too late for that.

Well, for now there is bright sun, and plans to make even though you're not in them anymore.

3/26/13

At the pond, the melting process has begun. Ducks paddle and bob near the bank, the muskrat travels under the ice, leaving a trail of bubbles, splashes away when she sees us.

But I'm not able to settle, and not sure why. Until I walk home, find a text from Lara, who says she is sick, needs prayers and good thoughts. "I'm not doing well," she says.

Oh, does caretaking never end? I heard a saying recently about parenting – that ultimate caretaking – "You are as happy as your saddest child." I would rewrite that: You are as happy as your sickest child!

A letter in the *New York Times* recently spoke about losing the people you've taken care of, and how it drags you down, how it leaves a large hole in your life, one way and the other, both when they're here, and when they're gone. Only someone who's been there – on that rough, impossible road of carrying someone else – can know what it's like. We are eaten alive. And still, don't want to be spared, because what would that mean? The end. The end, the end, the end.

A lonely, impossible, oddly graced journey this caring has been, and still is; never, it seems, really over.

There ought to be a place where caretakers can go afterward, to recover; collapse, breathe, without waiting for the phone to announce the next emergency. So far, I haven't found that. All my beloveds, in one way or another, need more. And you? I guess you don't need anything from me now. But the hole you left, the wound I fell into for so long, is still raw. I'm not sure what to do about that. For who would choose not to love? And love means being with – no matter what.

Well....for now the day ahead stretches out before me. There is beeswax melting on the stove for the new, big basket waiting to be sealed; Lara somewhere out there needing help; many school phone calls while

I'm writing; Bodi needing to walk. And just this moment, a life in the middle of care, scented with honey and wax.

3/27/13

After getting up at 2 a.m. to catch the bus and then the plane to North Carolina to visit my friend Sarah, I fall into a kind of torpor. I just can't be busy anymore. Even opening the computer, asking for hot tea to drink, is more than I can do. So I don't do anything at all. Stay folded up in a soft place, without thoughts, desires, a press to do anything. This is all I can handle, for now.

3/28/13 a.m. (*At Sarah's in Raleigh*)

Here I am, trying to tell your story. But it isn't mine to share. I can't claim you, or even tell the long, rich tale of your life. That belonged to you, and now it's gone. And maybe none of us can claim the journey we think is ours. We belong to the long, brave flowering of the world, unfolding one battered, stupendous petal at a time. Perhaps we can only hope to bloom in the small bright sun of a life, dance in whatever wind blows our way, dizzy with the wrenching joy of a little time and an overwhelming love.

I can't go back to what is gone. But your life still shimmers inside me. The tangled trail of our family still twines up all around. I am both what went before, and what presses its tenacious self forward, using this body as a home.

So much falls away. But some things stay. The gauzy, lively room we have made out of love is surely one of those.

3/30/13

Morning

Awake with antsy, eager thoughts about meeting Wayne Vial and his wife today. I want to make it warm for them, am swamped with a certain anxiety, an almost "cellular desperation" to be liked by this "new" cousin. What is this visceral hunger to belong? I really want to know.

Evening

Wayne feels like family. His stories overlap with mine. We both learn much.

He, too, has questions about why we didn't grow up neck-and-neck with all the cousins. We guess that our mothers were a bit overwhelmed with the "tribe," the noisy, raucous family gatherings. He does remember large funerals with everyone meeting back at Keet's, all the hugging cousins and aunts and uncles and "grands." I remember that, too.

He fills in some gaps, says the photo you had of "Papere" dated 1897 with some grandchild is Louis Adolphe Vial. The dates work, the planes of the face line up with the old picture I have of L.A. as a dapper gentleman. I fill in a few blanks for him, too: that Zo got her nickname from her father, who called her l'oiseau – little bird. Wayne never knew that.

So another friendly, curious bit of the big family puzzle, this time in the Carolinas, another southern place we have touched down and sunk roots. I think you would have liked meeting him.

3/31/13

I can't have your life, but part of me still wants it: the rumble-tumble brothers; play with so many cousins; the mad press of loving, friendly folk. If I had had all that, the early cloud of loneliness might have slipped away. But I could be wrong. For, looking back – which is most of what I've been doing since you've been gone – is a fractured, hazy vision at best.

4/1/13

On the ground in Baltimore, waiting for the flight back to Portland, I don't think about you much – and then I do. I am where you were. My heart still opens its doors, turns inside out. I could call Peggy to see how she is and to talk about you, but I don't. Sit, instead, squeezed into my too-little seat next to people I don't know. Soon, I will fly over your former home. How can it be, that I could come here without seeing you?

Oh, I love you. Oh, how much I remember all those hard and busy times and troubles. Little did I know about love; it could all be gone in the blink of an eye.

4/9/13

I wonder why you ended up alone, spent your life without someone who lasted years, decades, beside you.

You told me the short story: in those times, a woman had a husband and a homebound life, or a career. So you had to fly. But what about the longing, all the joy? What about skin that surged upward to meet an eager hand; the ways you were built to lean into familiar warmth— the curve of a shoulder, an arm around your waist? What did you do with all that – or, rather, without it?

I need to know, for here I am, doing life all by myself, too.

4/10/13

A short walk down to the pond on a drizzly, gray day; rain dripping off the trees into the water, a few ducks lazing over to check us out, a small time to sit before the many chores of the day.

And rumbling thoughts – about school, and choices, and riding the wobbly line between what might shore up my financial future versus just ambling through the quirky loveliness of my life. Which is best? How do I know? How do I decide anything alone? Not such an easy thing.

I wonder where you are now, but the question feels too translucent, too holy, to ask. How do we live in the middle of mystery, all the while pushing forward to the daily drum?

4/12/13

Is everything I do lately just another way of holding on? Going down to Louisiana, doing herb work, Mike, you – am I just wanting to feel comfortable, wrap myself up in familiar things? For what am I, after all, if I really let go? And what are you?

Is the love room only a dream made up of me, holding on? I think not. Surely, there is some of that. But your wrenchingly sweet and lingering presence seems to be real. And hard to give up.

4/16/13

Today, the Boston Marathon bombing.

People are broken in the streets. The world is shuddering. You are forever gone. And still – sun shines, a muskrat slides under the surface of the pond, new leaves have the courage to sprout.

Everything falters; everything thrives. Love breaks, and breaks open. I am wonder and fear, joy and rage, tears and hollowness and lush, ripe fruit. I am both brought to my knees, and racing toward a future as if it were sure.

Oh, how much there is to hold in our shaky hearts. Oh, how our love room with life is both warm and buffeted, shocking and sure. Oh, from wherever you are, show me how to bear all this, for I am a prisoner of irrepressible love for the world, crushed by care that tears me apart.

May we find mercy. May we bow down at the altar of life. May it be so.

4/18/13

In class today a woman talked about grief. She listed all the surprising symptoms: isolation; fatigue; lack of focus; anger; anxiety; mood changes; overeating; or not eating. Sleeplessness. Disconnection.

Yes.

I live here, in this everyday world, like everyone else. But I am also living in a place no one sees. The country of grief wraps around me no matter where I am. It still claims everything.

4/22/13 a.m.

Earth Day! Cold, at thirty-four degrees.

An email arrives from Nanette about visiting Hahnville. I am shocked again, overwhelmed, with how much love I have for that place and those people. Swamped with waves of longing and care, I want to be there. I want to go soon, and stay long. I want the roots of my beginnings, and the soil to which they clung. I want the arms of my family wrapped all around. I want to be home! If I can't have you, at least I can have that.

Are we born into and imprinted with an earthy place that settles into our cells? Never really slips away? I understand a little of what Native peoples mean when they say they *are* the land –inseparable from a place. Apparently, so am I.

4/23/13

Lately I am reading Emily Rapp's book on the loss of her baby son to Tay-Sachs disease, and on grief – the many ways loss gnaws away at those left behind. She offers a list of all the ways grief shows up. I find myself sighing all the way through. Sighing – one of the symptoms! Three whole pages of symptoms that become just the way we are.

Maybe the trick is to be careful about what you see, keep an eye out for that moment when you let the grayness slip in and get used to it, decide that it's just the way things are. Everything fades, everything falls away. The cataract of grief is still coloring my world, has become so familiar I can't remember happiness, or how to rise up and claim the energy for change. I am still hanging out on the edges of just giving up.

Oh, how do I give the love room, with all its real, mysterious, heart-rending beauty, the place it deserves without letting it take over my life? How do I claim the still-lively possibility of a future that is mine, and not yours? How do I keep living, really living, when you are not?

What do I do with the jumbled joy, the fierce passion for the world, even as it seems to fade? I don't think I can choose to let go. The love room has claimed me, and I am a willing prisoner, so far, though I am chafing at the bit after two-plus years. Surely, at some point, this has to be enough!

Are you there? Are you listening? Do you care that here I sit; still thinking of you, still leaning toward the hole you left? How do I move forward? Can I stop paying attention? Can I just lay the many flowers of my life at the love-room door, and then turn away? Will you be lonely? Will I?

4/24/13

I think I hear Bodi coming to jump on the bed, tussle pillows, play-snarl, nap. But he's still boarding at Happy Tails until I pick him up.

I miss the things that are gone even when I know they are coming back.

4/27/13

I hadn't thought of you, as something I'd have to fight against, but I'm starting to see this in a different light. Maybe, as much as I have been grateful for our space together, you have turned out to be tenacious. How do I break away from our sweet, leftover love so my life can bloom up? I am still alive; surely that means something. Surely, I am supposed to take up the still-being-created threads of the life that belongs to me, to me alone, and weave a new way forward that is willing, strong, and eager, curious and bright.

I wish someone could tell me this: how to live with the fierce love, the visceral grief, the awesome, holy mystery of loss, and still rise up out of my bed of ashes to move forward with any kind of joy.

4/28/13

Again, this morning, I am tired, thinking about how I carried you. How I spread out my life, and you climbed into the middle. How I grabbed the corners, cinched them up, shouldered your small weight for so long. How much lighter I expected things to be once you were gone. But I didn't know how heavy loss could be.

Still something new is happening, another corner turned in the direction of coming back to life.

Maybe I am coming to terms with some things: you, being gone. Me, claiming this motley bundle of ragged joys that seems to be my life. Loving, even when it tears my heart to bits. Maybe this time has been a womb: dark, heavy, mysterious. Maybe the wretched fact of losing you has been an incubation, a kind of birthing room into what I can still become.

Now, I sit in the light and shadows of Eleanor's camp. The woodstove breathes warmth. Bodi sleeps under the table. Mist rises up out of the hills across the road.

4/29/13

On Daddy's death day, I am feeling very low. Am I now going to grieve him, too, after all these years? Will the rest of my life be tinged with loss and letting go? My friend Cathy says that, after a certain point, life is all grieving and maintenance. You agreed, when I told you that. But I need to be happy! How will I stand a long road of faded joys without the people and places I love?

5/3/13

An at-home day in Portland, busy with good chores: some seedlings planted in the garden, a walk in the woods, the beginnings of a new basket.

Then, diving into your things; this time, a flower-papered box of old letters, mostly love notes from Papa to Grandma as they were getting engaged, then through the first years of having children.

"My own darling," he begins, and "Beloved." After years of life together, a few babies, there is still this – "Beloved" – written from work, on courthouse stationery so fragile I fear it will crumble. But it turns out to be surprisingly strong—like our family, I guess. He loves writing to her and waits for her answers.

Your notes are in there, too – a history of the Martin family as Keet told you the story, written on an old envelope. It is good to dig through, discard what might be trash, excavate what could be precious and revealing, begin the physical process of letting go. Sort out my present life from what has gone before. Except, of course, for what has taken residence in my heart. Which would be you.

5/4/13

A dream of the Upper Ridge house again. I guess the things I've lost will just keep showing up. My dreams don't know about letting go, and that's okay. I could dream of you, too.

5/5/13

Today the air is warm, comforting, close; wraps all around my body that longs so much for ease, for a little time out, for paying attention to the quietest of things.

It's an odd and tricky time. So many threads of my life, weaving together and unraveling all at once. I wonder how I'll manage the necessary details of doing everyday life and still claim gentleness – a capacity of heart – that has been wrung right out of me by too much work, too many pressing demands in caring for you all those years. I am worn out.

What will I choose for the future? I could continue to "do the details," work more and longer and harder, but what about the tenderness in me that longs to unfold? What about the roses of my heart that want to bloom, one at a time, in the hidden garden of joys? What about my own love room with life?

5/6/13

Today, Peter, who is now four and a half, wanted to come over to my end-of-spring-semester junky mess of a house. He insisted on a tea party, so we cleared a space on the table. He poured juice into a pot, cleaned up messes badly, then trailed after me into the yard, where he played in dirt but didn't want to get dirty. Then he raced off to the woods, leading the dog. He soon got tired of running. "My heels hurt," he said, which means he wants a piggy-back ride.

In the woods, we sat on a log to rest. He was afraid of newly hatched flies that buzzed around the softened wood, so asked to sit on my lap, climbed his long-legged self up, tucked his big head under my chin. His hair smelled like little-boy sweat; his cowlick tickled my nose. I tried to rub his t-shirted back, but had to be sneaky. He's not a snuggly kid!

Then he raced back away, wanting to be chased, and fell; skinned a hand, an elbow. I wanted to scoop him up, but he didn't want to be touched. We sat on the sidewalk in front of a neighbor's yard while he cried. I asked how I could help. "Just sit with me 'til the pain goes away," he said. So I did. I watched tears well up and slide down his blushing downy cheeks. Waited. He gripped his own scratched hand, cradled the skinned elbow. "It hurts," he cried, and rocked himself until, finally, the hand was better, the elbow not so bad. We talked a little. Then he was up, running down the street, daring me to catch him again. And okay.

At his house, though, he wanted his mom, let her pick him up, his Spiderman-sneakered feet bumping against her thighs as she carried him to bed, tucked him in with all his new yard-sale beanie babies, and stayed with him until he fell asleep.

I am learning so much these days, about what he needs, how to listen, how to love without grabbing on; about boys, and this particular boy; about how to lay down what I thought grandparenting would be – all snuggles and sweet surprises. Instead, here I am, a student of this inconvenient love, making a new, quirky connection that will turn out who-knows-how. For now, we are both showing up, and liking it a lot.

5/10/13

At the pond, geese still nest despite rising waters. This morning, the mother lifts up, fluffs feathers, resettles. The male hunches nearby, will help her out once the chicks arrive. She'll be hungry, though, by the time the eggs are done, and busy, shepherding babies all over their new world. And then a long flight home.

Everything pulls away, finishes, flies off. But here I am, not quite leaving so many things, including you.

I am still the student of the mysterious fact of love, of living and not living, of what to do with care when the one I cared for so fiercely is gone. How does one ever learn this impossible thing?

5/11/13

Walking this morning in a hard rain, and getting soaked. In the woods, I lean against a little tree for a moment, sniff its wet bark. It has no leaves, no branches, only one thin, tall trunk, stretching up.

This tree still has a love room with the sky. The habit of love, of reaching out, lingers long, I guess.

5/14/13

Today, on my way to acupuncture, miles away, I pass the frozen custard stand that is smack in the middle of a farmer's field, a tiny hut surrounded by all the newly plowed fields. And notice that they're open for spring. Today's flavor: salty caramel marshmallow – yum! But it's the black raspberry I want – the best! Once I've lost a few winter pounds, I'll be back, even though it's a long drive. If I can get you to come up, I'll take you there.

Oh!

The impossible wrench of remembering: You're not here.

5/15/13

Geese are still patient on the nest.

5/19/13

On the radio today, I heard singer-songwriter Amy Grant tell the story of helping her parents go through their end times – that rough, hard work of the million details, the unrelenting care, the heavy responsibility, doing it all alone. She complained to a friend, who agreed it must be hard, but it was something else, too. "This is the last great gift your parents will give to you," her friend said. The opportunity to care.

Oh.

What gift would that have been, for me? The chance to work hard, to get over myself, to push through the weight of wounds and what I thought I didn't get, and just give. To fight for you. To hold up your dignity. To dredge up, out of the bottom of my halting heart, as much love as you needed. To offer what I could. More than I could.

The chance to know you, not just as strong and remarkable, but person to person, heart to heart. To bear your tender vulnerability that needed a hand to hold. You gave me that. The work, and the chance to slip through your careful guardedness and into the juicy center of your heart. And into my own.

5/25/13

Two tiny Louisiana connections: an invitation to Emilie's graduation party (a big family fete at the end of June) and a short note from Nanette. I fold them up, put them on the top of the mail to read later. Another link to my heart, and to you.

I am making my own connection, it seems, to them, to that place. Does the love room make babies, then? If I have a heart-tugging tie with one person, does that spread out, give birth to other loves and links? I would imagine so.

5/27/13

In the woods, lady slippers bloom, star flowers are up and lush. And, at the pond, there are goose babies! Six tiny, pale-yellow balls of fluff, sailing along in a straight line between their much-larger parents, who keep an eye out for any errant strayling, nudge it back into the safety of the family parade. They trail over pollen-dusted water, clamber up onto the island to huddle in the nest on this first warm and sunny day. Turtles rest on the log; muskrats zip by, mouths crammed with leafy twigs; birds chitter.

So many things to love. How many days, weeks, years, have I sat on the edge of any water, watched things unfold and throb, then pull back in the colder times? And how long will I be able to do this: trek through mucky woods, follow rugged trails? At some point, maybe not so much. But these wild wonders will still be lodged inside me; have become part of my skin, my breath, the way I see the world. Just like you, I guess.

5/29/13

A crazy, displaced day; a frenzy of chores, then a walk to the pond, where only three of the goslings are left. The others were eaten by a snapping turtle, someone says, and two of the survivors are limping. Who knows what tomorrow will bring?

A few of us stand around and watch. We are a family of sorts, tied together with the place where we live, sharing care and concern.

Not so different from the love room. Everything we care about will be swept away. But, oh, the sweetness of having loved!

5/31/13

A hot day! You'd be so happy. Already at 7 a.m. it is seventy degrees. At the pond, fish flip into air that smells like lily of the valley and honeysuckle, damp ground and pond water. I lean against the tree, watch life squiggle all around me. My body is beginning to believe in warmth again.

A few sad thoughts this morning: a friend's daughter has just died after a long struggle with cancer, leaving two babies behind. And a co-worker's partner of eighteen years has left without warning. My heart is turned their way. So much loss, and pain. Yet here I am, in the midst of resilience springing up all around. Is one true, then, and not the other? Does this beauty negate the sadness, or does resilience somehow need the fertile ground of what has dwindled away, in order to rise up fresh again? Do they just live neck-and-neck, what is good with what is impossibly hard?

At the small back pond, the geese are thriving. Three babies still swim and dodge around their parents, a little bigger every day.

And I'll be going to Louisiana soon, will meet more cousins, and think about the possibility of living there, at least for a while. Will visit your ashy body's weird little cemetery home. I think you'll be hanging around, in the graceful trees, in the close heat, in the smiles and stories of our people. There'll be the pain of you not being there, and the joys of so many remnants of your life.

For now, there is the luxury of a little time to make these notes, to think of you, to send little airy hugs.

6/1/13.

I sit in the quiet bedroom. Tug your shawl up over the back of the chair, then stop. It might be time. With all the spring-cleaning chores lately, I could do this, too: shake out the shawl, fold it tenderly, pack it up, or give it away. Lighten things up.

So I try. My hands stretch out, draw back, reach out again. I whip it away, let sunlight pierce through slats in the chair that has been covered, now, for almost three years.

I like it – the lightness instead of the dark, even though the dark was beautiful. Still, I put the shawl back into place. Tomorrow, maybe I'll try again.

6/3/13

A dream about the end of the world, and deciding I could be saved by curiosity, by getting past the fear and paying attention to what I could learn from it all.

On waking, I think it must be true: that in the midst of the complications of life and the dangerous world of loss, I could be saved by wonder, by finding the beauty that swims all through the tragedy of grief.

Now, I sit in the rocker that is bare this morning, your shawl draped over the foot of the bed, fringe trailing to the floor. I can still reach out and touch it. My hand, my arm, so want to do that. Oh, if only the curve of your thin shoulder were underneath.

I am still loving you. My body is still expecting you to be nearby.

6/4/13

Alison's forty-fourth birthday – amazing!

And so much life today in the woods. Turtles trying to nest in the woodchip pile, a big muskrat leaping into the pond when we arrive, geese with two chicks left. First bugs swarm over the water. A heavy dew has settled in the woods.

At home, your shawl still hangs on the foot of the bed, but I'm not settled with this. Like the turtles who keep trying different sites for their nest, I am still trying to figure out where it belongs – where you belong.

6/11/13

A few thoughts about Louisiana and my upcoming visit. I am happy to be going back, but wonder about this seemingly endless hunger to belong.

Maybe I am turning back to them because they are the past – the living past, there, at the root of the root, grounded to all the lives that poured into theirs. They are what you were, what I might have been if I'd stayed. And now I want to go back.

One thing to remember, though: I am not just that rich and tangled past, the people we came from, the land we kept close – and neither were you.

6/13/13

I choose myself.

I choose the who-knows-how-long green road that only my own life can lay down. I don't know where it will end. Maybe it will meander backward, down South once in a while, curl into bayou territory before it straightens out into a new direction I can't foresee.

Maybe I am finally able to be born into this whole ripeness of my own particular life without you.

6/17/13

Afternoon

I drive into Hahnville, over the high bridge that is flanked by dark cypress trees hung with gray moss, in the swamping, sticky, bone-warming heat, over the river that goes so deep, curves so slowly, roils with hidden force.

I wonder how much is enough? How many times will I have to come back before I get what I need, which is – what, anyway?

Evening

Ice-pink sky. Much food and welcoming at Nanette's. Much fuss around the dog that will have surgery tomorrow. Cicadas chirring from trees all around, that chorus of so many childhood summer nights.

6/18/13

This place is becoming familiar – again.

At the river this morning, everything smells luxurious. I want to breathe deeper, longer, sniff it all up, as if spices and flowers, heat and mud and river water were all tossed up into the air along with time, memory, and a jumble of beloved things I could inhale: my dad, and you, all the brothers and cousins, the bloodlines and land and stories – every breath a taste of long-ago truth.

I think of you, coming here after all your siblings died. How strange was it to be back after they were gone, after Helen died? Did you walk down to the water that had swirled past all your earliest years? How hard was it, I wonder, to make what you must have known would be your last trip.

6/19/13

A long ride with Sunny and Nanette to the swamp at Lake Martin, to see the giant lotuses whose flowers smell like baby powder. Alligators slip past us. Roseate spoonbills, egrets, several kinds of herons flicker all around. Did you ever go there, into that luxury of hidden growth?

Halfway out toward deep water, we enter a deluge of storm. We get soaked, try to wrap up Sunny, whose rain poncho won't unfold. He gets drenched. We hunch against the wind together, slip into a little duck blind, wait out the worst of it, turn back early. Laugh and chat. In the car, Nanette turns on the heater so we can dry off.

I am saturated with Louisiana rain, and wild beauty, and family. We stop for warm cracklins to eat on the way back to the house. They fill me up.

6/20/13

Do memories have a scent? Do stories? This morning the air smelled like green dampness and so many flowering things, the ripening berries in a thorny thicket, dried cow dung in the hot sun, the hard-packed soil underfoot. It all smelled like home.

My eyes swept over the field, the tough, matted, snake-hiding grass, the hackberry jungle where you could have walked a hundred years ago, where your parents might have strolled to see their land before they were married.

I wondered about my house – the one I'm building in my head; will it be real? Do I want it? And why, and for how long? And what will happen to it after I've gathered up all the scents and stories I can stand? How long will I whip out this notebook, jot down whatever is happening and how it relates to you? How long will I keep coming back?

I don't know. But for now, I am visiting you, have brought flowers from Nanette's garden – pink and salmon and red – to the cemetery, such a strange and unwelcoming place. The blossoms are stuck in an old pickle jar, but I don't think you'd mind.

Today, in the immensely close heat and the noisy thrumming of the chemical plant, a green dragonfly lands, touches down tiny, prickly black feet above what's left of your bones, then lifts off. I think she is visiting you.

6/21/13

Tonight, a drive with "the cousins," as if I were one of them – which I am, but never was. They talk about Louisiana, the confluence of beauty and corruption. I ask how they keep from getting discouraged, when so much seems impossible to change. Dede says it is hard, but they do what they can. And some things shift over time.

Now, a solstice full moon, a big gray raccoon slipping through the darkened front yard, but no stars so far. Nanette says they don't see as many stars here as we do in Maine. How would I live in a place without stars?

Is that why you left?

6/22/13

Yesterday, one cousin talked about a local woman she had met and really liked. She described the woman as "so self-deprecating," as if that were a good thing. Could this be part of what you sloughed off? Maybe Maryland was far enough away, and academia liberating enough, to give you another way to be a woman in the world.

Maybe what Nanette called your "aloofness" developed as a way to push down that cloying closeness with all its attendant rules: be self-deprecating; bow down to men; and talk about food. You never even learned to cook; what a rebellion!

I wish I could ask you about these things: how you decided it wasn't for you; why you refused all of those men, knowing that if you said yes, you'd live the rest of your life as someone's wife, mother, helper.

You said no, and off you went.

6/23/13

Today, a busy, fun, noisy, crowded graduation party with our relatives – three graduates, three generations.

How much you might have liked this – seeing them all, catching up, laughing. I have so many photos of you, surrounded by relatives, looking so happy. It's like that for Emilie, who is graduating from high school – all she wanted, she said, was to be with her family to celebrate.

A great fullness, all these people; the ones here, and the ones already gone – Grandma, her sisters and brothers, all the aunts and uncles and cousins, going far back. A swell of quirky, feisty lives, a mess of stories – some happier than others, some easier. What must it have been like to grow up in the middle of all this? You tried to tell me. And now, here I am, getting a little taste of it, too.

It's a bit overwhelming. But, getting up to leave, I am overcome with sadness. Why do I have to go? Why do I have to do everything alone?

6/27/13

I'm glad you did what you wanted: sank slowly down into the silence of the end of your very long life. Remembering now those times when we sat and chatted, and then got quiet, I get teary; such a sweet grace.

I don't imagine you're remembering anything where you are; you must be beyond that. But maybe your memories have collected in the little ethereal pocket of all good things gone.

You are a good thing gone, still flickering by the love-room door.

I am still loving you.

7/4/13

Am I finished writing to you? How could that be? But what could I tell you that you don't already know?

7/6/13

A surprisingly steamy morning, for Maine. And a fall, a broken arm, then a quiet day. Lara picks me up to run errands; the stalled car is off to the garage; I have phone chats with friends, texts with cousins. Nanette calls to check on how I'm doing.

The figs are in, she says, so many they don't know what to do with them all. Bursting out of their skins. She will make preserves, use the syrup as a glaze when they smoke meats. Her pooch is better, up and eager to run, and Sunny is fatigued. Monica will come to check him out.

I want to hear all this news. I want to keep talking. I want to eat as many figs as I can, and go crabbing tomorrow with them all.

Here, now, the air is hot and sticky again. I want ice cream. If I were down South I would top it off with figs!

7/10/13

Home after a short walk through sticky, steamy woods to the pond where I tried to gather linden flowers for tincture, but one-handed, with a dog on a leash, and many of the blossoms too high to reach, was pretty hard work.

Near the pond bank, two night herons flushed up out of the brush. The geese sailed by with their single, now-almost-grown chick, which is just getting its final colors. A turtle sped up to check us out, only her nostrils showing above the surface.

At home now, I feed Bodi, make tea, think of you. I am afraid of what will happen if I can't write. You feel so quiet now, so far away.

7/13/13

What do I do with all your photos? I can't just throw them away! The long, bright record of your journey, of so many stories untold, has disappeared except in these faded scraps of what's left of your life.

I could share a few with family who knew you, I guess. Then each of us would have a handful: small snatches of you. Maybe you would like that, though at this point I'm not sure you would care.

But it's still a lot of work, sorting through all this. I don't know how much more I want to do.

7/23/13

I sit in the rocking chair, writing to myself, when your shawl, silky and cool, slips down over my shoulders, settles behind my back. It has ended up on the chair again. It seems to be at home – or I seem to be at home with it, which might be the same thing.

Last night I received an email from Nanette, catching me up on the news. Sunny is better; the pooch is back to her old, quirky, hound-dog self; the weather is good; Emilie is going off to school soon and Dede is sad. And the figs are gone.

A little taste of family.

I heard a woman talk on the radio recently about loss, about families, and grief, and how we get through. Relationships, she says, are complicated. But even in the hard ones, where edges are sharp and old feelings and unmet needs still linger, we are held together.

A family is a constellation, a solar system, she said. Each person moves in a predictable orbit so the system can stay intact. When someone dies, it's as if one of the planets just disappears – is torn out of its orbit – and all the other planets go awry. What we try to do then, she noted, is to fill the gap.

Hahnville, Nanette, Dede, Sunny, Mary Janet, and all the new cousins; the swamps, bayous, the back pastures, the cows and coyotes and June berries, the river; Jara and all the gardens; crabbing on the lake; the little weird cemetery, red navel oranges, the figs – they might all be place holders, bits of a new planet around which I am wrapping my orbit. When what is really needed, what is missing, is you.

7/25/13

At the cemetery, behind the community garden and the raspberry shrubs, I stumble on half of a dead dog, eviscerated. Its entrails stretched out, gray and slippery, across several feet of grass. A leg, not too far away Yellow tufts of fur dampened with dew and pressed into the grass. Grisly and jarring. Maybe death is always that way, no matter what.

Today's best news? I am out of my sling. My arm is healing, the doctor says, so I am using my hand, even though part of the arm still twinges.

My right hand can touch my face again. I can feed myself without losing half a forkful. I can swim. My parts are so happy to be back in touch.

Losing you has been a little like this: two parts of a whole that can't touch each other anymore. I have gotten used to it, but there's an emptiness my body still notices, a lack; one hand, missing the other.

8/6/13

Waking up this morning at Eleanor's camp to many beauties: a peach-colored dawn, caught and held in the shallow waters of the pond; owls, loons, veeries; golden dragonflies who pause to mate on a folded pickerel leaf, then flick away; feathery, filmy clouds in the great dome of the sky.

At the Owl's Head beach, I step into the cold ocean at high tide when the sunlit sand has warmed it a bit, watch an old yellow lab working on a huge rock under the water, his big-bodied dance to get what he wants. Which reminds me of you. Two years ago, I came to this same place to rest and recover after you'd gone, and watched another (or the same?) dog in a determined frenzy to dig up a buried stone.

All these things, my body remembers and loves, including, of course, you.

8/7/13

This morning Bodi and I walked through raggedy unmown fields that were heavy with dew, honeybees rising up from wildflowers in the early sun. At Eleanor's, there were boisterous dog greetings, and time for tea and chatting.

We talked about aging and what to do about the future, how to get our needs met, and about loneliness – the scary fact of bad things happening when there's no one to help. And all the responsibility, and who might share it as we age. And about grief, how to let everything go and still love the life you have. Eleanor said her sister is grieving after suffering a loss, is overwhelmed.

I remember the overwhelming part after you'd left. I think I am coming out of it now, though there is a limit to how much I can do without needing recovery time. Still, something of that lowness has loosened up, is coming to a kind of close.

This writing, too, might be rounding out. Here I am, at Eleanor's, where I came in those hardest times to take breaks from the work that was endless and all the phone calls that were scary. After you'd gone, I came here to recover, slog through the grayest of months. To wait for little touches of the love room, the sweetness and surprises of you showing up.

Here, the quiet pond lapping over itself, owls booming in the night, the veeries and osprey, eagles and loons, the ocean at Owl's Head, wide green fields, the wild silence – all teased something apart in me, helped soothe and soften the impossible truth of the end. Your end. Here, something was still good, alive. Lush, and trembling.

Now I paddle out over warm amber water, dip a hand into the pond, and somehow, maybe, the joy that wells up in my own life spills over into the well of all lives loved, especially yours. My life is still breathing into the love room, keeping you afloat.

8/9/13

I am looking back over the letters I've penned to you for almost three years, tracing the tender road that led to the love room door so I can see the whole map of our after-time together. I am searching for a pattern, to see how my life, that had loved yours so early, leaned into you when I was young and you were livelier, has handled this journey of loss.

Our time together seems more distant now, though still lovely and wrenchingly hard to lose.

8/13/13

I may be going to Nova Scotia soon to meet up with cousins Lennie and Kathi who are trying to follow the trail of our family. They think they've found a link to our Louisiana kin there, and they're off to explore. They wondered if I'd want to come.

It would be hard going – the drive, and all the things of my life I'd have to shuffle around. But these, the ties that bind, are also the anchors of my heart. Maybe if I get to know them better, they will be another little place my heart belongs, another "planet" in the constellation of our family that could help to balance out the hole you left. Good, though not the same.

8/14/13

Oh, how can I love you as fiercely as I have, and still want to be free? I want to tend to my own life for a while; isn't that okay?

Last night, poring over your old photos, I threw more away. Stiff bits of hazy history go into the recycling bin. Still, I am left with hundreds and, as much as my heart flares open when I see some laughing, shining shot of you, it's a bit too much.

Maybe I can sort through what's left and hand them over to Kathi and Lennie. They can take a turn, see what triggers the sweet chain of their own memories. Can have what they want, because we are all you have left now, and there's only so much of you each one of us can save.

8/17/13

In Digby, Nova Scotia, with Lennie and Kathi after a dinner of scallops right out of the ocean, warm rolls freshly made, salad just in from the garden, an innkeeper who sings to us while we eat. A late sun that burns and blushes into the bay.

Earlier, Kathi took a picture of me and Lennie on the High Hill stones where the road winds up over granite boulders and spruce trees hold up the sky. I look happy. I always look happy with family.

Now, in the next room, the cousins pore over a chock-full file of old pictures. Firecrackers pop against the darkened sky across the bay. The tiny refrigerator hums in this spare and comfortable room. I hope to sleep well, and to be up early enough to walk and run and get oriented to this place before the cousins wake, because even though I am learning to love them, even though my face is smiley-happy in the photos with my arm slung over Lennie's shoulder, I still need time alone. I am like you in that: both companion and loner, family member and monk.

One thing we learn, as we tell tales about you tonight: We are a motley crew of independent creatures; that's for sure!

8/19/13

After a long day of tracing family roots through small-town archives on a meandering drive, we look at the photos you left. They should decide what they want, I say. Lennie asks for some favorites; I hesitate, then say OK. But one goes, and I want to snatch it right back. It feels so wrong. I am shocked at the twinge, at the longing that – even though I said I was tired of it all, and done – still washes over me.

But it gets easier. Why shouldn't Lennie have some? A few years older than me, she remembered you before I could, loved your whip-crack smile – the dimples – the flash of something bright. We see you in the arms of different men. We wonder who they were.

And she takes very few, really. We bundle what's left back into the folder for me to take home. "It's a big job," she sighs. Yes; you left me so much, and so much to do. I am still holding the thin-shelled egg of the whole of your life, wondering what to do with it all.

8/20/13

Riding to the ferry dock this morning with Lennie, we have time to talk about our lives as single mothers, and about family: what we loved; what we had to overcome; what you were to us. A spark, Lennie says, that we both turned toward like flowers to the sun. In the dark confusion of mixed-up parents and alcohol, we had to go toward a certain kind of light, and you were that.

We talk about grief, and about our brilliant, sometimes quirky family. Last night we swapped stories about the drinking and the wild times. And about why Papa stopped drinking. We each knew one part of that story. Her part: that Grandma had a very hard, long labor with my dad, was in danger, and when the doctor sent for Papa, he was "on a toot" – somewhere drinking. No one could find him. Once he showed up, she says, the doctor gave him hell.

And the piece I know? That he had the hired man lock him in a shed, pass in food through a window, not let him out for two weeks, ignore whatever pleas or threats he might dish out. And that was the end of drinking for him. Lennie says that later, when there was a family party, Papa stayed "dry." Oddly, though, his level of excitement and laughter ratcheted up right along with that of anyone who was imbibing. The habit of exuberance, of rip-snorting raucousness, lingered. The rush, the high, never disappeared.

8/21/13

Did sharing those bundles of pictures with cousins help in any way, lessen the sharp impossibility of you being gone? I guess not.

More of the chat with Lennie seeps back. We are both the children of your happy attention, still kneeling at the love-room door. I can't say how it was for Lennie, but I have little doubt that I wouldn't have made it through the numbing, ragged trials of growing up otherwise.

Will missing you last forever? How do I let anything go? How does the world keep moving on if losing even one person is so wrenchingly hard? How do I get my mind, my heart, to leap over this – the abyss where you used to live? Impossible.

Now, Bodi is happy to be home – sleeps pressed against my leg, his soft ear flopped over my knee. His breath makes a little damp spot on the satin comforter. Some things last for a while, I guess; habits, and small loves.

8/22/13

Night birds twitter outside the window, cicadas ring from the trees, broken-diamond bits of the starry sky shine. Another summer day. Another day without you. Another day with the love room fluttering all around.

8/26/13

If the soil under my feet, the air pressing over my skin, settles into tissues and bones, slips into my psyche, colors how I see the world

– how could anyone ever really be gone? How could you be gone? How could all out beloveds just disappear?

Here I am – almost three years later – still asking that.

8/27/13

I'm back at Eleanor's camp again, thinking of you as your death day anniversary comes around, that sacred day you slid into the forever Mysterious. If your every leaving-day will be holy, and your coming-in day, too, what does that mean about the rest of the world? Could the coming-in and the going-out days of every beloved be sacred? And what about all the creatures of the earth: whales and ponies, bears and orchids, the cypress tree finally fallen, the first crackling shell of the snapping turtle, the last blink of a lion, laying down its fierce and graceful life? What about the cerulean sigh of glaciers, leaving their trail of aqua tears? Surely, every coming in and going out is a grace, stunning and raw.

What if we remembered that? What if we woke each morning, already bowed low at the altar of all things cherished? Would it be easier, somehow, to let my beloveds go, if I remembered that I am breathing souls, that every in-breath is a love room with the world? That every out-breath is, too?

Could this be it, that not one speck is ever really gone? That life holds her delicate children – all of them – in her gigantic, trembling heart, forever?

I'm not sure if that helps, but it might.

8/29/13

Tonight I am loving the owls and their raspy, throaty calls, a sky that sizzles with stars, crickets ringing all around the house – and having waited for you. Whatever rough edges this – the love room – has pressed into the tender tissues of my life, I am nothing but glad. Some happy chance has landed me at the love room door, and I have stepped right in.

9/1/13

At the house, Eleanor is ironing. We chat and have tea – lonely, older women, leaning toward each other.

Then a wet walk back to the camp. Bodi is especially wild, races in crazy spirals through the sodden, brilliant woods, ends up wet and filthy. He eats voraciously, can't seem to settle. Me, either. Chores and the trip home are already niggling.

It's so hard to leave. But, even though I am reluctant to go, this place will stay with me, keep quenching some thirst in my life. It will become me, in a way, just like you have.

9/2/13

Almost three years that you've been gone. Time really does take you away.

9/3/13

Tomorrow, the third anniversary of your leaving day. The acute, shattering realness; will it never stop? Do I want it to stop? Is it possible to love too much, or too long?

As all the hours of the day tomorrow flutter down to your leaving time, I will wish to spend them in quiet, just holding the gentleness of your having-been.

One good thing – Peter will be five in a few weeks. He is tall, still reserved, but impish, too. He talks a lot. And he is getting to like bugs. His dad finds one outside when I'm there, and we pass it back and forth. I am holding surprising things – rust-colored wireworms, hairy white caterpillars, and daddy-long-leg spiders – because I don't want Peter to be afraid.

Last week, at school, they painted his hair pink and blue. He thought it was hilarious.

I hope you know these things. He is such a joy.

9/4/13

At the beach, the sea has disappeared and the mudflat stinks of fish. Here's what there is at this, your leaving time: pain. I hate that you're gone. I thought it would get easier, but there is still this at the heart of it all – you're not here.

Now I know why I come to the ocean, to beaches, on your last day. I can stare out into the nothingness, which is what is in me: the flat, wide landscape of loss, the useless, empty land once the water is gone. Boulders, bereft without the sea. The grudging sky.

I am both happy to be alone, and unbelievably sad. But anything else – anything cheery, or chatty, or even comforting – would just be wrong on this, the emptiest of days.

Loss is hungry. It gobbles you up. It takes everything. How sad can a body be, I wonder, and not give up? How can we all walk around as if everything is whole, when so much is missing? I am demolished. There is no escape. Not reading. Not doing three loads of laundry in the small time between class and appointments. Not chocolate. Or the frenzied swim in cold water as the tide slips out. Not watching the sun shift through the sky.

How can I let the truth be its grizzly, velvety self, and not just fall down on my knees every single day without you? This breaking apart seems endless. Like you said near the end, this is just too much.

If you were here now, I would sing to you. I would tell you the dahlias are beautiful this year –slow to start, but glorious. And the cicadas are back. And I guess my life is okay.

But I want what we were. I want you back.

Min traveling with
friend

Min with young family
members

Min in Egypt

Year 4

Coming to Ground

9/5/13

Are all these little letters my way of not letting you go? I want to be with you. I want to hold up the love that cannot fade, even when the person does. So there is this trail I am laying down, this packet of notes: small, rounded pebbles of patience you could travel across if only you would.

9/13/13

I had thought this would end, me waiting for you.

9/15/13

Yesterday was my mom's death day. Fifteen years now without her. Easier, in some ways, painful in others. Suppose she had lived longer? Suppose I could have seen her as just herself –one feisty, uncertain woman on the curious road of a life? Suppose our hearts had been able to touch – one real mother to one real child? What if I hadn't been afraid?

I was motherless long before she was gone.

Why is it I could have that touching of hearts with you, and not with my own mom? And now you're gone. You're gone, and she is gone, and that's that.

Suddenly I am sobbing, wrecked. This, the primal loss, has been hiding behind you all the while. Her absence slipped behind yours.

Does that mean I never cared for you? Or were you just the easier door into what needed to well up so I could be free? Easier – though wrenchingly hard – to lose?

In the midst of sobbing tears, I feel your smile. You have held the door open so I could find my way back to this, the original loss.

Why am I surprised?

9/29/13

Another report on the state of the world: weather and climate (definitely changing); islands (in danger of disappearing); fires (many, and out of control); money – who has it (the few) and who doesn't (most everyone else); greedy power blocking any meaningful change. We barely know what to do, and what we do know seems too much, or not enough at all. In my turbulent storm of grief and aging, and coming to terms with hard things like you being gone, I hadn't planned on this.

Losing you was one terrible thing. Losing the world? Unthinkable.

10/10/13

Dark night, with hazy new moon.

I miss you – or, rather, I miss missing you. At least before, when the loss was so raw, you felt closer to me.

10/11/13

Last night at a small gathering I talked with a co-worker about the love room and this jumble of letters written over three years. She was curious. She is losing her own parents, bit by bit, as they age. Her eyes gleamed with hope and tears, which made me want to work harder at pulling it together – this chronicle of what it means to love and to come apart, not because you chose to, but because it's just the way life is: here, and gone. Lately, all I want to do is sit with the bulky, messy packet of notes, capture what it means to pay attention as caring unravels over time, show that these – the thready, silky scraps of leftover love – can be both ragged and good. Enough, when it's all you have left.

10/13/13

This is what I would talk with you about, if you were here: how to sink into the juicy, jeweled brilliance, the fierce, wrenching fire of loving the world even though everything will be swept away.

10/14/13

I sit at the window, in the sun, watch light fall on downy, thick leaves of the African violets, silver the tiny hairs, light up wine-colored petals of flowers.

I think of you in your last years—of how you would sit, just watch the sun and shadows slip across the wall as dust motes quivered in the lit-up air. I think you were loving the world. I am doing that, too.

10/19/13

Walking in the gorgeous, burnished autumn woods while sunlight hangs in trees; paling pine needles flutter all around; a confetti of colorful leaves lies underfoot, fallen.

Fallen.

Do love rooms end, grow thin, breathy, give themselves over finally to the Great Passing By? Surely the doors can never really close, for what love could ever not have been? But each and every thing under the sun must have its own time – flare up, flower, fade.

Soon I'll be going back to Louisiana, to Hahnville, to sit with our people again, talk, eat, rest in the warmth. I'll be there on the date – November 4th – when we gathered together for your family funeral, buried your ashes, and they welcomed me back into what now feels like my tribe.

I am coming full circle, it seems. I am able, in small snatches, to trust the world. I can join in the fray, be one more motley, spicy speck in the quivering soup of a life. Does this mean I am laying you down?

Is this what you were waiting for, through your long, long time of keeping watch? You, one lucky flash of the Great Generosity, always turned my way?

Now...wild geese overhead, many honking voices, on their way south. Home.

10/29/13

Waking to thoughts of what to do with the big fern I can't seem to give away. It curls high over my head from the corner near my bed, losing leaves so that every morning there is leaf litter in my hair when I get up. Me, still holding on to things, I guess.

A little email arrives from Nanette. Amazing how much it matters to me – the sweet thought of going down there, to our people. There'll be a party, she says, on Sunday: football and family and food. I'm not so interested in the football, but everything else will be good. I'll be thinking of you.

11/1/13

A long All Saints Day in Louisiana, two meals eaten out – (catfish, crabs, crawfish, shrimp, fabulous onion rings). And much chatting and catching up. Fun, and overwhelming; bits of stories I try to piece together, still learning names and details.

At Sunny and Mary Janet's, we sit outside in the warm evening air. Hummingbirds nudge at feeders newly filled. Oranges and satsumas hang heavy on tree limbs. Mosquitos sting our ankles. Cousins talk about fighting oil companies who wrecked acres of cane fields and are still weaseling out of paying for clean-ups. My cousins are warriors for the land.

Now, the sky is dark, church bells chime, boats hoot up from the river. What would it be like, I wonder, to live shouldered up against that gigantic, throbbing stream?

11/2/13

Nanette has spent the day getting ready for tomorrow's feast: smoking meat, chopping up what goes into the jambalaya. We share more stories: all the currents of family; who loves whom (everyone, of course, over time); who is "out of the box"; who is happy, who not-so-well; who has to struggle more; who is comfortable.

11/3/13

Morning

I get stuck in the mud, trying to take pictures of three egrets on a log, then climb over the levee to watch the river tugboats push barges as the sun comes up. Back at the house, Nanette is cooking already, preparing for the big family feed.

What would you be doing now, if you were here? Not helping to cook, for sure. Maybe getting things ready for the kids or walking a little by yourself. Later you'd be laughing, catching up with old friends (who are cousins, too), a drink in one hand, an arm slung around someone's shoulder.

Well...here I am, instead, getting ready to soak it all up.

Evening

A fun time today; good food, little kids, many cousins newly met. The best thing? Playing chopsticks at the piano with Mary Ann and Coo, all of us working hard to get Patrick (a child prodigy, they say) to play for us, which doesn't work, but we laugh and hug and have a great time.

Today's news flashes:

- Sunny is feeling quiet and tired, but shows up later to say hello;

- The fish in the aquarium all died at once after the tank was cleaned yesterday. Everyone is sad, and trying not to let the kids know;

- Tom loves doing pottery, has a special bond with little Brittan, who is three. Tom carries him around while Brittan drifts off to sleep. Tom smiles and smiles;

- Emilie is home from school, has a banged-up knee, is going to study law, she says—another lawyer for the tribe;

- Mary Ann is sharp and funny – she reminds me of you;

- Will is sixteen, getting taller, nuzzles his dad, who ruffles his hair and hugs him back;

- Celeste brings four desserts that are completely gone within minutes of hitting the table;

- The dog has a big night – gets two bones instead of one;

- Outside, the air is colder; a planet breaks through the river-fogged sky.

Back at Nanette's house, she and Dede, after cooking all day, eating and sampling wine, stay up til 1 a.m. in the kitchen, pickling onions. Dede peeling, Nanette measuring vinegar and spice, talking about family and friends. "We are the fun cousins," Dede says, and I agree.

Maybe I can stand this, after all – you being gone. In our people, I see little flecks of you everywhere.

11/4/13

Morning

On the river beach, I walk barefoot over cool, powdery sand as light seeps into gray sky and the air throbs with bird chatter. I am thinking of you, and our tribe, and the close, busy jumble of us all. Did you notice? Lately I am thinking "us," instead of "them." This is how it is to belong, I guess; good, and sometimes a bit much. In a place where, in every direction you turn, there is someone else's story, liveliness, need, how do you hear your own voice? I'd always need to slip off to someplace wild and quiet to empty my head, so chock-full of other people's lives. I'd need breathing room.

Still...at Nanette's there is more chatting, because this is the heart of the heart, the bank of stories, the original love room, and I can hardly get enough.

Afternoon

After a fun foodie lunch with Pete, Dede, and Nanette (fried pickles with red beans and rice), I am off to the cemetery, to bring flowers and to sit with you.

Three years ago today, we all gathered here for your little bone-resting ceremony. Now, in the sun and wind, I don't feel so sad, but I don't want to leave, either. Even though my mind says I'm okay, my body still wants to bend low, hunch over, kneel on the ground. How can I tear away?

There is no answer. Life is full of holes. Grief is real. It lives neck-and-neck with joy. The emptiness packed right in there with the brave, honeyed busyness of everyday life. There is no getting over it. I am living the awesome, awful truth of life and death, all woven together. Complicated, multi-layered, and not all of the layers are sweet.

If Nanette were cooking, she would say you have to pay attention, take your time; one layer, then the next. In the end, the flavors seep into each other, settle into something nourishing and rich, each effort different than the last.

Here, now, the sweetness runs through me. You are still with me in some way I don't understand, but willingly drink up. Oh, the happy truth of it all.

11/5/13

Up early to catch my flight, with hugs from Nanette, nuzzles from the dog, the lovely, breezy warmth of southern air.

At the airport, I get stuck on the wrong floor of the rental car return, stop to ask a large, gentle black woman for directions, which she gives, sweetly, and I start to cry.

Here's what I have found: after growing up on the edge of loneliness, being a very young mom and the leftover wife of a mean man, there is you, having gathered me up and carried me along, and family. My people; they care for me.

Who would have thought that, after all that time of taking care of other folks, including you – some great emptiness that has hollowed me out for all my years could be healed?

Is this my inheritance, then, a final gift from you? A new love room, flush with the motley crew of our tribe, warm and quirky, complicated and fun? Will our love room – yours and mine – come to rest in this new and comforting grace: the family I leaned toward as a child?

Who knows what I'll do in the end. I might decide to come back, take a chance, find out whether or not I belong to all these ways of warmth. Or maybe I'll do what you did: visit, stay for a while, soak up the goodness of kin, then retreat back into the well-worn turf of my own life, away.

No matter what I choose, though, it seems that my love rooms are merging. Maybe all love rooms intersect in the heart, nest inside each other in the small, shiny mess of any life. My love room with you, all fluttery-airy and pale these last few years; my earthy link to this lush and gorgeous land; the new, sweet, and quirky place I am building with little Peter; my love rooms with daughters, friends, and now the entire warm and crowded whole village of our people –becoming one.

Where will you be in my future? I don't know yet. But now, you are right over my shoulder, listening in. Probably that will always be true.

12/6/13

Back in Portland, at the pond, Bodi and I sit together on damp pine needles, watch rain fall into dark water. We have grown into each other. I am his "normal"; he is part of mine. Our love room is still intact.

12/8/13

Yesterday, while I was driving Peter to the park, he sat in the back seat, watching out the window and singing to himself, counting numbers up to twenty. He asked me if fifteen was 1, and then 5, and I said yes, and he added that to the song where he had left it out.

It's such fun to watch him take things in, get all wrapped up in curiosity and learning. Church, he said (as we passed one), is where people go to pray to God, and God lives up in heaven where the angels are.

I haven't asked him yet what he thinks God is. I'll probably try to slip in a few of my own thoughts: God isn't necessarily a man; God is in us, too; everything is a little bit of God. But I'll have to be sneaky. He has definite ideas about what he thinks is right. He keeps a sharp eye out for mistakes, and has no problem saying what he thinks. He is like you, in that. You'd love him to pieces.

How many times have I told you that?

12/10/13

We walk over ice-crusted snow after the storm. In the woods, crows rise up out of trees in a noisy, black cloud.

Near the pond, one of the marriage trees has been marked with a rounded splotch of bright orange paint: the logger's sign. Sometime soon, one of the trees will go.

But what about the poetry of it all, the mysterious twining of two trees, who have leaned into each other for so long? Why not just leave them to their lives, a reminder for those who pass by of what it can mean to love? To lean together, to stay both solitary and utterly willing to share a life?

Maybe I just don't want anything to change. Can't stand the thought of any more loss. What will it mean for these trees that have grown into each over 50 or more years? One will die. The other will be left, bereft.

12/12/13

You are still inside everything I do, it seems. Inside the bubble of my life, every hard, or strange, or happy, or curious thing. My mind – the data bank of keeping up with things – knows you're gone. But my body, this map of my whole life, doesn't believe it at all. Still leans your way. Such a marvelous pain. I don't know if that will ever go away.

12/15/13

A long walk in the new, deep, sparkly snow, eighteen degrees with no wind. Walking is hard work, but worth the effort. Sun gleams through dark trees, shimmers in a hundred thousand snowflakes on the pond.

At home, a note from Nanette. They are nine hams short, she says, for the Christmas baskets. A few years ago, the cousins started gathering food every winter for needy families in the community. Their original goal was ten. This year, the goal was forty-five, and they've gathered fifty-one. She is storing the meat in her fridge; as usual, she is the bank of nourishment. But she ran out of space, so she'll pick up these last hams today, and get them out to folks.

Oh, I so want to go there, want to be part of that warm throng of cousins doing good together in that home place. I guess we always want to go where we were first loved. I need something to lean toward; it used to be you.

12/21/13

Nothing replaces you. Despite my new love and longing for the Louisiana clan, the hole you left stays empty. How could it be any other way?

12/22/13

In the love room, surely who we are is formed, at least in part, by who the other person is. Like grains of sand pressing against each other, we are both shaping and being shaped.

What will happen to me now, without you to grind me into place?

12/25/13 Christmas

Five degrees this morning, icy roads, with a small wind. Treetops shine with sun on ice-glazed limbs that clack together overhead. We skip the long trek to the pond, though later I will miss the quiet time.

At home, getting ready for people to come for Christmas, my heart is very full. I so love being with family and friends: the warmth and generosity and even the crazy, busy, frenzy of all the work.

Sweet tears gather just behind my eyes. You would be so glad to see us all: Alison, happy in her new home, where deer sneak into the yard from the woods; Peter, playing with his million toys while his dad teaches him about numbers, ("I need a block with six knobs and a slanted side"); Lara, so glad to be with her new guy, who is gentle and attentive and kind; and Celeste, who has made $900 this past week baking pastries and treats.

I love you. I miss you, though not in the same harsh way as before. What we made together can never be replaced. But love is love. It all comes together in the end, in one throbbing, busy heart of a life. Today, here we all are, carrying you forward into our future, even though you're gone.

12/26/13

Even though our love room seems to be coming full circle, and part of me wants to "package it up," say: "Yes, these letters had a beginning and now, an end," I can't imagine not writing to you, not having you flicker up at the edge of any ordinary day.

Last night I talked with Nanette to wish her Happy Christmas and to keep in touch. She was just getting back from busy holiday gatherings and glad to be home, though with a new, achy cold. All the cousins gathered tonight at Alicia's for a feast that Nanette was too tired to attend. Her mom got a new car for Christmas, tied up with a giant red bow on top; a surprise from the family. Only the third time in Nanette's life she has seen her mother cry. And Dede is grumbly with Emilie home, but okay.

Small touches of connection are good. But what about you? Gone. That is still the truth.

1/8/14

I hope I'm not closing the door as this writing is winding down. But I have to take care of my here-and-now instead of leaning back to you.

I know you'd understand. I think you'd be happy for me. But I don't know how to think of myself without you. I don't know how this works. I hope I can have us both. I'll keep listening for your little whispery sighs, will probably see once in a while small flashes of you in the ways I love the world or ponder over things.

I have to hope so.

1/14/14

Can I really give you up?

As this process comes around to a kind of "closure," whatever that would be, I am so grateful for this time – this bubble of easing toward the end of the end.

1/16/14

What will happen to the love room if I retire and move away? So much of our after-time-together was "born" here. Me, standing in the weathered late-summer yard, stunned with the raw, new truth of you being gone. The first gauzy reality of loss and mystery coalescing. The love room giving birth to itself.

But surely our roots went deeper than this one place. There was Maryland, and Hahnville, the Upper Ridge house in Maine where you came to check out my life; all the places we knew together.

I still have so many questions. Mystery does that: leads us deep; wrenches us open; takes us by surprise.

1/28/14

As we swing toward your birthday, and mine, I am wondering how to make an open door into the love room so it can be shared. How to offer this diamond truth, both spangled and sharp, of what lies beneath the ground of our everyday days, pushes toward the surface with the earthquake – the life-quake – of loss. How to beckon a wanderer into what seems, at first glance, like low and dangerous ground, but turns out to be a rarefied place – a grace I might not have known if I hadn't been forced to go.

And so I have. Part of me is still loathe to give that up.

1/30/14

Bodi is lost in the cold woods. Or not really lost – he knows where he is, hunkered over some wild, torn-apart dead thing, chowing down. But he is lost to me. The space around my body, where he ought to be, is empty. Funny, how palpable emptiness can be. I can't stand it, am panicky. I walk on, double back, call and call. I am undone.

Finally he comes, mouth chock-a-block full of frozen, fatty bone, his wolf-self so proud. I try to pry his jaws apart to take it out, but he won't budge. So we walk to the pond, his body trembling with cold from the shadowy, ten-degrees woods. His feet are frozen. He lifts them up, one at a time. I take off gloves, hold a paw in my warm hands until it thaws, doing this thing that love does – trying to help, complaining all the while.

"I was so worried," I say. "I'm so mad!" I make him heel, and finally, when he gets tired of walking with his mouth half-opened and sets down the bone, I scoop it up, toss it away. He keeps looking for it, sniffing everywhere the leash will allow, but it is gone. Like I thought he was gone. Like you really are: gone. We all avoid the emptiness, search for what has disappeared, try to fill the space.

It feels good to have him back, even though he made me mad by leaving. And you? There's no getting you back. But I see a little bit more of what has wrapped all around me without you: a palpable emptiness, a lack. Nothing about it makes sense, at least not to my body – which is, of course, where I live.

1/31/14

Lately I'm reading more memoirs of grief to see what people have said about this rarefied time when we (those of us left behind, and what's left of our beloveds) still show up, somehow together, still hanging on.

There are some interesting observations: sleep changes (check); dry mouth (check); sinus issues (all those tears, waiting to be shed); and a "romance" with the lost one, so much brighter than the prickly, tedious chore of loving someone who's alive. Well...I guess I have been doing that with you, with all these little notes left at the love-room door.

But what is real, anyway? Even the sharpest intellect, the bravest soul, might feel the presence of the beloved after they're gone. Isn't the web we make together real? Isn't the rupture a loss? Wouldn't part of us still be intertwined, and regret the tearing away?

Another note – that the more people who share the loss, the gentler it becomes. There are more folks to hold up the "presence," and the absence, of the beloved. Could that be why this is so constant for me? I am carrying you, and your loss, mostly by myself. And could you be insistent on leaving a little footprint on a heart – specifically mine? Could you have worried you'd be forgotten?

One more important point – that the survivor, the traveler of that gray desert landscape, has to finally choose to live, to fling open a door, a heart, to what is still here. What courage that must take. But also common sense, for who could stand facing a whole life that was gray, drab, half-hearted?

Can I let the silky love-room walls flutter around my shoulders, catch my eye, and still walk toward what is mine alone?

I hope that your way forward, if such a thing exists, is gentle and kind. I hope you can settle into rest. I hope you are swimming in love – that gigantic, quivering sea that is so much more than we know. I hope you can see that I'm happy; that things are okay; that I still love the world, even though you're not in it anymore; that my breath still sighs with love for you every once in a while.

But I am choosing the end. Choosing to lay this down, wrap it all up. I don't think this will shut you out; but it could move me toward what we were always about – the deep and thriving resilience of following what's real. I still want to live. I have lessons to learn, hands to hold, mornings to love. Skin and organs and thoughts. I am something you're not anymore. Here.

2/1/14

After a cold walk in the woods, a little thrill: browsing homes for sale in Hahnville, just out of curiosity, I find two or three nice ones. Huh! My body still leans in that direction. What could that mean?

2/4/14

Today, I think about calling my friend Kathryn, whose mother has recently died, to ask how she is. But I still hesitate to speak, to say anything real about loss, as if words would shatter something. Break right through. If I keep my mouth closed, the sweet loneliness stays intact. If I hold the sorrow inside – a slippery, bitter pill that refuses to melt – I might get to keep you.

2/5/14

In the night, I think about my mom again, remember what had almost gotten lost: that my first love room is still broken. Yours was gentler, sometimes awkward, but we could love each other without fear. My love room with my mom is still complicated, kept at bay, a bit of a wreck. Some love rooms aren't so easy, I guess.

2/7/14

How do I say goodbye?

Even though I said I was done, I would miss the bubble of writing to you. The bubble of our togetherness, the knowledge that someone (which would be you) would care that I am reaching deep, turning my heart inside-out.

Still...a real love room would need to keep growing in order to thrive. Like any living tissues, it would have to be fed. As much as I feel your love still drifting all around me, no matter where I am, how long could this work, if I am the only living one left? If the blood that feeds the delicate tissues of care flows only on one side? Surely, I will have to let go.

2/9/14

A long walk to snowy woods where milky sun seeps through clouds and over bright new snow. Then home to tea-making, window-sitting, dog-tending.

Bodi's eyes squeeze shut in a tired sleep. I snuggle close while he sighs. I have made a promise in this, our teensy love room, to keep track of him, offer what he needs. This is what love does, what commitment does, even if it is only with a dog. Intimacy promises to stay close. Maybe that's what my love room with you has been – me, having promised to stay close, and now trying to peel the tissues of your life out from under my skin.

I will lose Bodi. I have lost you. But the gifts of learning to love, even though everything will end, are worth it, I guess. For who would have passed up the chance to open up and care for someone – or some dog? Who would have passed up love, even if it smells like doggie breath and snow-damp curls?

2/10/14

I started out writing to God, and have ended up talking to you. Did I get the two of you confused? Were you so early my brightest light that I took you in deep? Did you become the star I leaned toward? And what happens now, if that's true?

2/14/14

So much has come along with loss: an exquisite tenderness, the raw shock, a primal sweetness, disbelief, the wrenching work, the many questions that have welled up and spilled over into this small space of our time together since you've been gone. On this Valentine's Day, my heart is so grateful for difficult joys.

2/15/14

Can you be so lonely you'd give your life just to belong? But what about being free? And what does it mean to want both – a place of your own, and the thick jungle of comfortable loves?

Louisiana; I seem to be throwing the anchor of my life in an old direction just to be close, just to sink back down into what used to be good. I am choosing the togetherness I drank up long ago, but from a small and fractured cup. I think going back will quench my thirst – and even the thirst of my daughters, who were hungry, they say; who grew up ragged and poor and now will get to belong.

2/16/14

In Hahnville, there is a little house. It shoulders up against the levee, leans toward the river. There may be hawks. There will be cows to watch, and horses, and trails to walk, and owls in the oaks. I'll be able to swing right by Sunny's office, past the old mercantile store and the barbershop where Mr. Archange, almost a century ago, left home to stop by your house one morning and found a new baby born. He took out his camera, the only one in town, shot a photo I have lost, but that is engraved on the eye of my heart. Your mother, body still large from pregnancy, holding up my dad at three days old. Her face turned, not to the camera, but down to kiss the baby's small head. I could go there every day, if I wanted to. I could step back.

Oh, your life is still a long, curious tunnel I am walking through. I don't know if this is healthy, or smart. Probably not. But something calls to me. I might be listening.

2/18/14

Morning

Snow moon shines through a blurry haze, full, at 5 a.m.

On your birthday (106!), I wake up thinking about my mom, and about acceptance – what she didn't seem to get much of, at least not from me. I wish I had given her that. I wish I hadn't pushed her away.

In loving you, in racing back to warmth and welcome, I am wishing it for her too. Maybe I am trying to heal what was broken and still needs repair. I don't know. But the fond, sad hopefulness, the love for my mom that somehow got blunted and closed, seems to be opening up.

Love. Love opens me up. If I let in one love, all the others flood in, too. The love room, both private and unique, and also the doorway into all loves.

Happy birthday, Little One. I am so grateful. Little did I know you'd be the doorway into healing my hesitant heart.

Afternoon

A crazy flurry of small miracles: A call to Nanette, asking about the little house there. She's a realtor, it turns out. Just showed the place yesterday. She liked it a lot. It needs some work; the floors were 'soft.' But it's a sweet place, she says.

I hem and haw; am thrilled, and terrified. Decide I can wait, and let the idea settle, see how it feels over time. Then she calls back. My name is first on the list of potential buyers, just in case it's what I want. The person next in line plans to tear the house down, put up a Dollar store instead, use the land for a parking lot. They will sign papers tomorrow. If I am really interested, I have to sign today, before 5 p.m.

And "Yes" comes right out of my mouth. Nanette can fax the papers to me, she says. I can sign and fax them right back. But I don't have a fax machine, will have to drive to work a few miles away, send it from there. And it's snowing like crazy outside; we're having a blizzard, snow falling so fast the plows can't keep up.

I do it anyway. My car is the only one on the road. Seven or eight inches of snow grab my tires, pull me side to side. My little mental tirade about how crazy I must be drones on and on. I finally make it to work just in time to discover that school has closed, the building all locked up tight due to the storm.

Tears streaming down my face, I call the agent in Hahnville, who, it turns out, lived in New England once. She understands. They can give me one more day.

But...can I really buy a house I've never seen? Then I remember that Lara is on her way to Louisiana to visit Celeste, who will pick her up at the airport in just a few hours. They'll be passing right by Hahnville on the way back. I make a few calls. Nanette will meet them at the house, so they can check it out.

And they both say "Yes." They agree that it's a sweet place. They can imagine me there. Nanette says we can start the inspections right away.

Wow. Am I really doing this?! Maybe I can try it part time for a while; be a "snow bird," spend winters in the south to see how it feels. Surely all these crazy events falling right into place must mean something. And oh, how I long to be there!

2/27/14

In Hahnville

I'm afraid that, in coming back to Louisiana, this time on my own wings, I could be losing you. If this place will be mine, do I need you anymore? If the little girl, who waited so long to come home, arrives, what happens to all her dreams? Oh, how the body reaches back. If I were Buddhist, I would say that I am attached. It would be true.

2/28/14

Morning

On my sixty-seventh birthday, waking to dreams, and the train whistle, far back in the field. Last night, we all looked at Nanette's gorgeous book of photos from Queen Bess Island – the so-intimate details of pelicans nesting – spiky clumps of feathers, yellow mating plumage, blue eyes. The fleshy, naked curve of a baby's wing.

Land. Home ground. Here I am, doing ridiculous, complicated work to get a place of my own. There's really no going back, but here I am, pretty close.

Evening

Tonight, dinner with Nanette, Lon, Sunny, and Mary Janet. Sunny tells the story – hysterical and crazy and true – of spending his whole day at the office with loud, ceaseless security-alarm blaring, spiders triggering the signal, no way to get it to stop, a lost fix-it man, computer crashing, phone repairman who can't fix the phone, but sits down and repairs the computer instead, on and on – a whole day of this! We are all laughing. Nanette says later that our family is full of good storytellers. I agree!

3/1/14

I am stepping back into the skin of the past, after all. Like the thin green moss that covers anything here that stands still, it has gotten into me.

3/2/14

Here I am, loving some things you might have done: biking yesterday with cousins along the levee to see the small-town Mardi Gras parade. Then everyone pitching in to work on Sunny's new potato bed while fire ants ring my ankle with small, pimply bites.

Even the hard things are welcome. I am taking them on – the fire ants, the big trashy river, the whole neglected state.

A new, capacious love room where you still float; the stunningly sweet breath of our togetherness still quivers. I still love you.

3/3/14

Leaving for Portland again, I wonder how this was for you, going down to be with family, and then traveling back to your home. It might have been a relief and a sadness, all mixed up together. They are easy to love, hard to leave – as you were, too.

3/12/14 *In Portland*

I've slipped into the sad habit of talking about you – as if you were a sweet thing of the past. Which is true.

3/23/14

My friend Suzy was here for a few days, up from New York City, where her mother died just weeks ago at age ninety-seven. Suzy sat with her for the whole week before her death. Her mother – never easy, got a little softer toward the end – was not the least bit worried about leaving, not resistant at all. She was ready to go.

Now, Suzy is sad, wakes up crying. "It's going to be a weepy day," she says. Some days are like that. She drives around in her car, crying, talks on the phone and her breath ends up in a sob. Tears slide down her cheeks.

But she doesn't mind. There's something going on she can't explain. And she doesn't want it to stop. In some way, even though her mom was difficult and distant, they're still together. Suzy is both here, and not here – still somewhere else, with her mom, and she doesn't want that to end. Doesn't want to try to explain, or be cheery, or pretend anything.

I understand. I tell her a little about the love room – about where I have hung out with you for so long, and how important it has felt for me to give space to this, the unfolding of the end. She cries again, "Yes, that's it exactly."

I guess I am standing, at least a little, on the other side of the crevasse of loss now. Loving the sweet room fondly. Beginning to gently step away.

3/27/14

My head is full of Hahnville thoughts: wanting to be there now, wanting to fix everything in my new house – floors, walls, foundation, on and on. How good it feels to be working with Nanette, who could run a country! And how happy Lara and Alison will be to come down there once it's fixed up – to get warm in the winter. Little Peter will get to know his Louisiana cousins, and maybe ride horses. He'd love that.

I wish I could tell you all this. I wish I could take you there.

4/2/14

Back in Hahnville again, I walk with Jara as she shows me her jungly garden. She knows all the plant names, the natural history of the land. Even though it is still daylight, an owl calls. We follow the sound over blackberry brambles and prickly cleavers to stand at the base of a tree, stare up into the big bird's chocolate eyes. Jara waves. The owl answers. We are happy, standing there together.

4/3/14

Swamped by sweet living memories, just under my skin, behind my eyes, of all the things I leaned toward as a child: wild tangles, the slightly scary mystery of hidden places, dark water, rustling brush.

Now, here I am, feet touching back on home ground. A visceral good. I could do anything: take a boat into those bayous, tramp through woods and mucky mud.

I could find you, and my dad, and all the things I both had and didn't have.

5/20/14

A busy day of work on the house, then cherry picking with Nanette and her mom. No time for a cemetery visit, though. Do you miss me? Are you sad that I got too busy to come? Do you understand?

And do you love my little house? If you were here, at the old place where you grew up, and time didn't have to happen in a straight line, you could visit me. You could walk right down the road, check out the new paint, make Cherry Bounce. Eat shrimp and okra with Nanette and Celeste and me.

That would be so good.

6/29/14

Do you see me happy? I wish I could give this sweetness to you, serve it up on a platter so you could nibble at these – the small homey joys of an everyday life.

I don't know if they would matter to you, but whatever is left of your heart, any fondness you might feel for this funny, stumbling world, might want to know that it still works this way. Even in the midst of struggles, things are lovely. Even in the face of pain, beauties abound. Even in the truth of loss, there is still love.

Mamere Martin's house (Min 2nd row, far left)

Min's parents, Jean Baptiste Martin and Leonide Vial Martin

Epilogue

Epilogue

One day I thought you were there, and then you were gone. You were taken away. But still you lingered, hung like feathers in an upward breeze, and taught me this:

the end is hell
the end is promise
the end is not the end
all our beloveds live on
grief is an open door
you can step through

Now, having lived with your end that was not the end, I am turning around, starting to face forward, and wanted to offer this – one small, sweet gem of the after-time for anyone else caught between worlds, between now and then. Here, and gone.

In charting each step of these after-years, maybe I've laid down a map – small footsteps of a lurching heart after the firestorm of loss. Some have been sweet; some grueling. Some, pressed so close to Mystery, I could barely breathe. Some, lost, even though I've tried to keep track.

All I can say now is thank God – thank the luckiest of graces. Thank you for being here until I had planted the roots of this, my gnarly spangled work of coming to ground. Thank you for lingering at the love-room door.

Who's who in the love room

After my aunt's death, I brought her ashes home. There, in the small Louisiana town where seven generations of my father's family had been born and raised, I met numerous cousins, some of whom I am related to on both my paternal grandmother's and grandfather's side. All the cousins are in some way directly descended from two large and interesting families that grew up woven into each others' lives through marriage and community life.

When I was a child, my father used to say he was related to everyone in Hahnville. At that time, he was probably right. Now, names have changed, faces aren't always familiar, but our tribe of a family continues to live in and to preserve an increasingly rare, and always necessary, community of care.

Cousins mentioned in the letters include: Sunny Vial (Leon III) and his wife, Mary Janet; Nanette Vial (Mary Janet III); Dede (Francesca) Vial, her husband Pete Schneider and children Emilie and Will; Jara Dubroca Roux; Mary Ann Vial Lemmon; Tom Vial, Lon (Leon IV) Vial; Coo (Christina) Vial Comer; Alicia Vial Molaison; Cary (F. Charles) Martin; and his father Fred C. Martin, all of whom live in Louisiana. Out-of-state cousins include Lennie (Leonide) Martin Gortner and her daughters Kathi Bonnabel and Dorothy Heathman; and Wayne Vial. Also mentioned is my paternal grandfather's sister, Keet (Marie Katherine) Martin Labry (deceased). Celeste Martin is my sister. Alison Adams and Lara Anderson are my grown daughters. My grandson is Peter Adams. Cathy Grigsby, Mike Corrigan, and

Eleanor Hansen are friends who live in Maine. And Bodi is the best dog in the world.

Acknowledgements

Many thanks to all those who offered support and comments through the long unfolding of this book. Joan Hunter and all the writing group friends heard the letters as they spilled out; Mike Corrigan first noted that I was writing a book; Deb Harlow loved it from the start; Lara Anderson cried all the way through; Cathy Grigsby, Chris Salem, Barbara Grandolfo, Jennifer Frick, Jacob Watson, Beverly Lanzetta and many others encouraged me as I waited at the love room door. Editor Shirin McArthur cast the first kind and constructive eyes on the manuscript. DeeDee Heathman and editors at Made For Success Publishing helped bring the book into form. Family members Nanette Vial, Leon and Mary Janet Vial, Jara Roux, Francesca Vial, Wayne Vial and many others opened doors and hearts, and supplied the nourishment that fed this project.

CPSIA information can be obtained
at www.ICGtesting.com
Printed in the USA
FFOW04n1028220218
45196261-45752FF